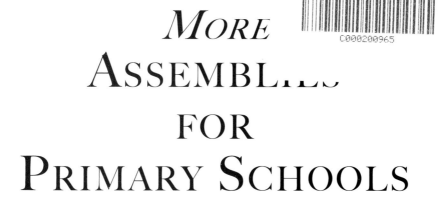

More ASSEMBLIES FOR FOR PRIMARY SCHOOLS

∾

AUTUMN TERM

Margaret Cooling

RMEP

Copyright © Margaret Cooling 2008

Margaret Cooling has asserted her right under the Copyright, Designs and Patents Act, 1988, to be identified as the Author of this Work.

The illustrations in the Appendix may be photocopied by the purchaser or the purchaser's school/organisation for use within that school/organisation only. They can also be downloaded free as a PDF file for printing from RMEP's website: www.rmep.co.uk/autumn The photocopying of inspection copies is not permitted.

First published in 2008 by RMEP
13-17 Long Lane, London EC1A 9PN

www.rmep.co.uk

RMEP (Religious and Moral Education Press) is a division of SCM-Canterbury Press Ltd.

A catalogue record for this book is available from the British Library.

ISBN 978-1-85175-356-7

Designed and typeset by Topics – The Creative Partnership, Exeter

Illustrations by Clive Wakfer

Printed and bound in Great Britain by Barnwell's of Aylsham

Contents

Assemblies by group

Group E **Making a difference**

Group F **Early scientists**

Group G **Poetry assemblies**

Group H **Changing children's lives**

Group I **The way of St Benedict**

Group J **Sweet assemblies**

Group K **Luke Street**

Group L **Advent and Christmas**

Alternative themes index

Harvest

Hallowtide

Advent

Christmas

Easter

Prayer and reflection

Virtues and values

Faith in action (people and charities)

The world around us/scientists exploring the world

Ourselves

Acknowledgements

The author and publisher thank the owners or controllers of copyright for permission to use the copyright material listed below. Every effort has been made to contact the holders of copyright material but if any have inadvertently been overlooked, the publisher would be pleased to make the necessary alteration at the first available opportunity.

Extracts from 'What is Truth?', 'The Golden Rule', 'The Love of Money' and 'Conscience' taken from *I Was Only Asking* by Steve Turner, published by Lion Hudson plc, 2004. Copyright © 2004 Steve Turner. Used with permission of Lion Hudson plc. Extract taken from *What Will You Wear to Go Swimming* by Lois Rock, published by Lion Hudson plc, 2002. Copyright © 2002 Lion Hudson plc.

The author would like to acknowledge *Prayers Encircling the World*, ed. Robert Keeley, published by SPCK, as the inspiration for prayers on pages 15, 19, 21, 28, 35, 42, 44, 49. The prayer on page 15 is based on prayer 207 by Joanna Cofie, Gambia © Mother's Union; the prayer on page 19 is based on a prayer 62 by Pamela Wilding, Kenya © SPCK; the prayer on page 21 is based on prayer 145 by Desmond Tutu, originally published in *An African Prayer Book*, published by Hodder. The prayer on page 28 is based on prayer 135 by Janet Nyenda, Uganda © Mother's Union. The prayer on page 42 is based on prayer 87 by William No Richards and James Richardson, Kenya, originally printed by Uzima Press, Nairobi in *Prayers for Today*. The prayer on page 44 is based on prayer 33 © the Indian National Industrial Mission. The prayer on page 49 is based on prayer 286 by the Justice, Peace and Integrity of Creation Women's Workshop, Tonga, 1987.

The author would also like to acknowledge *Finding Sanctuary* by Abbot Christopher Jamison, published by Orion Group Publishing, 2007, from which she drew inspiration for the assemblies on pages 55–64.

The prayer on page 85 was adapted from a prayer of North India in *Born Among Us* (USPG/The Methodist Church).

With thanks to David Edden for the music on page 92.

Introduction

This book contains 70 'broadly Christian' assemblies for use in primary schools (ages 5–11). In England and Wales, the term 'assemblies' applies to the non-religious items such as the notices and recognition of pupil achievement, but here it is used to cover the religious element (collective worship) as it is still the most commonly used term.

Brand new assemblies

This new series of assemblies contains fresh material for today's teachers. Inevitably, a few themes reoccur, such as the Easter and Christmas stories, but very different assemblies have been built around them.

Four nations

These assemblies can be used by all four nations of the United Kingdom. In Scotland several assemblies can be combined to create a longer act of religious observance. For details of legislation of collective worship and religious observance see the following websites:

England
www.dfes.gov.uk
www.teachernet.gov.uk

Wales
www.collectiveworship.com
http://new.wales.gov.uk/topics/educationandskills

Scotland
www.ltscotland.org.uk/religiousobservance
www.scotland.gov.uk

Northern Ireland
www.deni.gov.uk

Broad Christian tradition

The material in this series of books draws on the breadth of the Christian tradition: from Quaker to Catholic, from the early Christians to modern aid projects, from African Christianity to Aboriginal Christian insights.

Multicultural

The assemblies draw on Christian examples from around the world. The majority of Christians live in the two-thirds world (formerly known as the 'third world') and these books reflect some of that change in Christian demographics. For more information see: M. Cooling, *Rethinking Spirituality: An Approach Through Christian Spiritual Traditions* (The Stapleford Centre).

Spirituality

Some of the assemblies draw on a variety of Christian spiritual traditions so that pupils can see the range of spiritualities within one faith. For more information see: M. Cooling, *Rethinking Spirituality: An Approach Through Christian Spiritual Traditions* (The Stapleford Centre).

Values and virtues

Each book in this series contains a number of explicit virtue/values assemblies, such as 'happiness' and 'forgiveness', as well as general assemblies that deal with virtues and values. These can be part of a wider programme to build a school ethos.

Variety

Assembly themes are varied, covering charities, saints, values, festivals, biography, science, Bible stories and many other subjects. This is deliberate, as it allows as many staff as possible to be involved. Most members of staff should be able to find something they are comfortable delivering.

Seasonal

The books have been organised into three seasons to help people locate seasonal material. Some schools operate on multiple terms, but much of the material can be delivered at any time. Up to twenty assemblies in each book are seasonal, but even some of these could be used on other occasions.

Creating a programme

The material in this book can form part of a larger school programme of assemblies. The nature of the school – whether church or community, perhaps – will decide how many of these Christian assemblies are included in the programme.

Series

Most of the assemblies have been written in series of five so that they fit a school week. These series could, however, be split and assemblies put together in different combinations. Some suggestions are given in the Alternative themes index on pages 5–7.

Order

The assemblies are not necessarily presented in the order in the term in which the subjects occur. They certainly do not need to be delivered in the sequence they appear. The 'Luke Street' assemblies, for example, by their nature include both Christmas and Easter material. As suggested above, teachers can pick out individual assemblies from a series to present at an appropriate time if they wish.

Layout/fonts

Instructions and directions for teachers are shown in this font.

Direct speech, to be addressed to the pupils, or something the pupils might join in saying, is shown in this font.

Assemblies cannot be completely scripted. Teachers will need to improvise around the direct speech to make the assembly appropriate for the age and aptitude of their pupils.

Historical heritage
Some historical content is included to familiarise pupils with the Christian heritage of Britain. Well-known saints, and saints associated with particular regions, are the subject of some assemblies.

Using images
In some assemblies it is suggested that images are used. If you have the facilities for using web images this will enhance the presentation, but such suggestions are always optional. Please check copyright on images that you plan to use.

Pastoral issues
Some assemblies deal with sensitive issues. These should be handled appropriately and adapted to your situation as necessary.

➢ Halloween is a controversial subject, so an All Hallows' Eve assembly is included instead. This assembly looks at the Christian focus of this festival.

➢ Death is touched upon in some assemblies, for example, the deaths of certain saints. It is up to teachers as to whether they mention this or omit it. The Remembrance Day assembly needs careful handling if some family members have been injured or killed while serving in the forces.

Miracles
Miracles are the subject of some assemblies, and these will need sensitive handling, particularly healing miracles. Miracles for Christians are about power and compassion and often come from a relationship of faith. They are not magic, which is about control. Miracles are understood within Christianity as signs pointing to the nature of God and Jesus, showing the power of the creator. Christians believe that, as creator, God has the power to temporarily suspend the 'rules of nature'. Christians differ in their attitude towards miracles; some believe in them while others do not. With younger pupils, concentrate on the motive for miracles (usually compassion) and miracles as signs, and do not overemphasise the supernatural element.

Prayers and reflections
Both prayers and reflections are included, so that teachers can choose what is right for their school – either or both can be used if appropriate. Pupils should only ever be *invited* to join in prayers, never *forced* to respond. One option is for the teacher to introduce the prayer – if they choose to – by saying:

I am going to say a prayer. If you wish you can join in with the Amen at the end. Or you can listen quietly. Amen means 'I agree'.

If you wish you could ask pupils (ones who would be comfortable with this) to read prayers.

A range of activities are used for prayer and reflections, sometimes active and fun, at other times quiet and thoughtful. Text shown in bold is for pupils to be invited to join in and say together. This may involve displaying the prayer in some way.

Some material draws on prayers from around the world. The originals were used as *inspiration* only, as the language was too difficult or long for the school context. The following books are sources of prayers that can be adapted:

Prayers Encircling the World (SPCK, 1998)
A Procession of Prayers by John Carden *(Cassell, 1998)*
An African Prayer Book by Desmond Tutu *(Doubleday, 1995)*

Websites
Websites referred to in the text were live at the time of going to print. The websites do not necessarily represent the author's views. Please check copyright before you download any material.

Participation
The assemblies have been designed with participation in mind, and may involve pupils, other teachers, and school staff such as caretakers and meal supervisors. In some assemblies other community members and parents could be involved. The participation has been designed to be manageable in the context; either a few children are invited to take part, or all pupils do a small seated activity such as sign language.

British sign language
Some prayers and activities include signing. For this British sign language has been used. Signing is deliberately included to widen access and raise pupil awareness.

Health and safety
All activities must be carried out with due regard to health and safety, and teachers must act with reference to their health and safety documents. The lighting of candles should be done by adults, and candles should stand in a pot of damp play-sand.

Preparation
These assemblies are easy to deliver but they do require some preparation and there may be some items you need to collect beforehand. You could delegate safe elements of preparation to older pupils, such as creating a 'pass the parcel'.

Assembly box
It is helpful to have a box containing basic items that are often needed for delivering assemblies. The assembly box should contain:

➤ Scissors (child and adult)
➤ Stick glue
➤ Paper (different sizes and colours including large sheets)

- ➢ Card (different sizes and colours)
- ➢ Felt pens/pencils/crayons
- ➢ String
- ➢ Rubbers
- ➢ Post-it notes (large size)
- ➢ Sellotape and double-sided tape
- ➢ Roll of lining paper or frieze paper

Each assembly begins with a 'You will need' section that lists specific items needed to deliver that assembly. This list does not include the contents of the assembly box, which are taken as present.

Printing the illustrations
Some assemblies require large versions of the illustrations in the Appendix. These can be photocopied and enlarged or they can be downloaded free as a PDF file for printing from RMEP's website: www.rmep.co.uk/autumn

Bible quotations
All Bible quotations have been paraphrased to make them accessible for the age group. The reference is given if teachers want to look up the original.

Music
Music is suggested for some assemblies. This can be obtained from music libraries, high street music stores or on-line outlets and resources.

Presenting Bible stories
Bible stories and stories from the Christian tradition need to be introduced carefully so that both staff and pupils feel comfortable. The following form of words might be helpful:

Today we are having a story that is important for Christians.

Today's story comes from the special/sacred book of the Christians, the Bible.

This leaves everyone free whether to identify with the story or not. They can silently respond in their own personal way:

That's my story; we read that at home. We have that story at church.

Now I know why that is important for Christians.

It is important that pupils feel free to make their own response to the story, as long as it is respectful.

What makes a good assembly?
A good assembly needs four things:
- ➢ Content
- ➢ Atmosphere
- ➢ Reflection
- ➢ Participation

The following factors are also helpful:

- ➤ Pay attention to the general ethos of the school and relationships, as this affects everyone and everything.
- ➤ Plan the way pupils enter and leave; this can set the tone.
- ➤ Create a relaxed but secure environment. Assemblies need an ordered atmosphere but the discipline does not need to dominate.
- ➤ Avoid having distracting noises, such as the clattering of pots and pans.
- ➤ Think about the way the room is arranged. How comfortable can you make it?
- ➤ Make decisions about the presence or absence of members of staff. If staff do not attend, what message does it send?
- ➤ Separate the notices from the act of worship, if they take place at the same occasion. Create a ritual for ending one and beginning the other. You might use music, light a candle or have a stilling activity.
- ➤ Create a focus for worship. You might use a candle, a picture or some flowers as a focus.
- ➤ Use poetry, music, art, drama and silence as well as speech.

The happiness bag

You will need

A cheerful coloured bag filled with some of the items for this
and the next four assemblies.
The words 'delight', 'contentment', 'joy' and 'happiness' written on cards and
placed in-between the layers of wrapping of a 'pass the parcel'.
Some music to play 'pass the parcel'.
A jug of water and a plastic cup.

Introduction

Ask pupils to guess what might be in the bag. A few pupils can feel the bag and
pull out the items one at a time, saying what they are. Place all the items on the
table and explain that they will be used in the week's assemblies. Ask pupils to guess
what the theme of the assemblies might be. Place the items back in the bag.

Core material

If pupils do not guess, explain that the theme of our assemblies is going to be
happiness. **Happiness is an important word and most of us think we know what it
means but maybe there is more to happiness than we think.**

Play 'pass the parcel' with the prepared parcel. Explain that what is in-between the
layers is some more information about what we will be exploring in our assemblies.
Pupils and staff can take part. As a card is unwrapped, hold it up and read it out.
**In the Bible, happiness is made up of many things, such as contentment, delight and
joy. Each of these are attitude. Sometimes things happen to us to make us happy or
unhappy, but we can also decide on an attitude of happiness. Some people seem to
have little and are happy, others seem to have much but are unhappy. The difference
is attitude.**

- **Happiness is doing the right thing.** *(Psalm 1:2)*
- **Delight in all the good things God has given you.** *(Deuteronomy 26:11)*
- **Be content with what you have.** *(Hebrews 13:5)*
- **God fills me with joy.** *(Psalm 16:11)*

Reflection

Pour the water into the glass and ask the pupils to think about being filled with
happiness. In order to be filled, the glass has to be empty. We have to give happiness
away to others and be refilled.

Prayer (OPTIONAL)

**'Jesus, you were a friend to children, we give you our thanks for all you do to make
children happy.'** *(Based on a prayer from Gambia)*

Contentment

You will need
    Adverts (see Introduction).
    Biblical quotes (see below) written on coloured card or paper.
    Small gift bags, or just fold wrapping paper into bag shapes.
    Beauty cream (optional).

Introduction

Ask a few pupils to take the adverts out of the happiness bag. **Many adverts tempt people to think that they will be happy if they have certain things – the latest car, toy, clothes, or beauty cream that makes you look ten years younger.** Option: bring in your beauty cream and put some on yourself. Ask if you look ten years younger. Wipe it off again. **Adverts are always telling us that we need more. If we have this toy or wear these clothes we will be happy. All these things might be fun, but lots of 'things', or even being beautiful, do not make happiness certain. Often people find that when they have got them, they then want more.**

Core material

Place the biblical quotes in small gift bags. Invite some pupils to pick a verse and read it out or an adult can read it for them. What is the message of each verse?

- **Better a simple meal with happiness than a party in an unhappy house.**
  (Proverbs 17:1)
- **Let's not always be envying one another.** *(Galatians 5:26)*
- **Be content with what you have.** *(Hebrews 13:5)*
- **If you are content with what you have you are truly rich.** *(1 Timothy 6:6–8)*

A contented person does not constantly want more; they enjoy what they have. It is easy to spend so much time wanting the next thing that people forget to appreciate what they already have. St Paul, a famous Christian, said that he had learned to be content whatever he had. Sometimes he had lots, at other times he had little. Contentment is a gift that we often forget but it is part of the secret of happiness.

Reflection

Ask pupils to think about what they already have that they can enjoy (possessions, people). Suggestions can be written on cards and placed in the gift bags.

Prayer (OPTIONAL)

Pupils can contribute their own short prayers and add to the gift bags. Or read the following:

> **'God, the great giver, we pray for the gift of contentment; teach us to enjoy each thing to the full.'**

Delight

You will need
> Items with the word 'delight' in the title e.g. 'Angel Delight', 'Turkish Delight'.
> A long strip of paper.

Introduction

Ask a few pupils to pull the 'delight' items from the happiness bag. Ask pupils what they have in common. **What does the word 'delight' mean? Delight is really enjoying something, relishing it, taking pleasure in it. It is noticing the sensations and taking time to really enjoy them. Often we rush about so much we don't take time to notice what there is to delight in. Delight is:**

- **Sucking chocolate slowly so that you really experience it.**
- **A cat rolling on its back for a good scratch.**
- **Curling up under a duvet on a cold night and feeling its warmth on your skin.**

Ask pupils and staff to describe some other 'delight-full' situations.

Core material

Delight, in the Bible, is experiencing the pleasures God has put in the world. It is enjoying life to the full without harming oneself, others or the planet. In the Bible there are lots of celebrations and parties which people are told to enjoy. Delight is enjoying people, as well as the world, to the full. For believers this includes enjoying God's company.

- **Delight in all the good things God has given you.** *(Deuteronomy 26:11)*
- **With your families eat and delight in the good things you have worked for**. *(Deuteronomy 12:7)*

We, too, can take time to delight in the world and the people in it. This involves making the effort to *notice* that we are enjoying things. This is much harder than it sounds. Maybe we could share at the end of the day some of the delights we have experienced.

Reflection

Ask pupils and staff to think of the different things they can delight in and what they could look for in the day to take conscious pleasure in. For example, sitting next to a close friend sharing good news, tastes you enjoy, the patterns sunlight makes on the ground.

Prayer (OPTIONAL)

Write the words 'Thank you, God, for:' on a long strip of paper and ask pupils to suggest things they delight in to add to this opening. This creates a long prayer that can be read.

Happiness

You will need
> Two pupil dancers – one with butterfly wings (optional).
> Pair of sunglasses with sad mouths stuck on the lenses (cut from sticky parts of Post-it notes).
> A butterfly made from coloured paper cut as wings with a straw for the body.

Introduction

Prepare the dance beforehand, in which a child chases a butterfly that keeps fluttering away just out of reach. Then the child gives up and stands still, and the butterfly settles nearby. Alternatively, enact this with a paper butterfly. **A famous writer once said:**

> **Happiness is like a butterfly, the more you chase it the more it flies away, but if you sit still it may land on your shoulder.** *(Nathaniel Hawthorne, paraphrased)*

Core material

Most people really want to be happy, but happiness is one of those strange things, the more you reach for it, the farther away it can seem. However, there *are* some things we can *do* about happiness. We don't have to *wait* for things to happen to make us happy.

Lots of things could make us happy, but we just don't notice them. It is as if we are wearing unhappy glasses and only see the bad things. Put on the unhappy sunglasses. **We need to put on our happiness glasses and see the many things that could make us happy.** Reverse the mouths on the sunglasses. **The most important of these is people.**

People think that all sorts of things will make them happy – money, fame, an important job. In the Bible, happiness is rooted in relationships – in people and friendships rather than things. That does not mean that other things cannot be enjoyed, but they are not the *root* of happiness. Getting relationships right is the most important thing. For Christians, happiness is rooted in friendship with God and others.

Reflection

When we focus on making others happy, we sometimes find that the butterfly of happiness has landed on us. Use the BSL sign for happiness as pupils reflect on this. (www.britishsignlanguage.com, www.learnbsl.org)

Prayer (OPTIONAL)

Prayers can be suggested by pupils and written on the paper butterfly wings and displayed.

> **'Help us, God, to focus on the people that really matter to us, and to put friendship with you and others first.'**

Joy

You will need
- The letters 'J', 'O' and 'Y' written on separate small cards.
- Child-safe bubbles (teacher only).
- A candle (in a container of damp play-sand) and matches.

Introduction
Give a few pupils the letter cards 'J', 'O' and 'Y' in the wrong order, and ask them to create a word. Can they suggest words that have the word 'joy' in them? For example, 'enjoy', 'joyful'. Write the words up on a large sheet of paper. What have they got in common?

Core material
People often think that joy and happiness are the same, but there is an important difference. Things happening to us can make us happy or unhappy. Ask pupils to suggest things that can make us happy. The teacher can make suggestions for things that make us unhappy.

This is also true of joy. Things can happen – often unexpectedly – to make us joyful. Joy has been described as an unexpected guest. Joy is also something that stays deep inside us even when things are difficult. That is what makes it different from happiness.

Joy can be very bubbly and funny and exciting. We can feel like jumping for joy. Pupils can do this.

In one of his books, C. S. Lewis described joy like a tree covered in big, beautiful, shining bubbles. Blow some bubbles – away from the pupils.

Sometimes life can be difficult, but there can still be a quiet joy, deep down, that helps us through those stressful times. It is like a candle flame in the dark that refuses to be put out. Light the candle and ask a pupil to blow it out. Relight it, and repeat the process. Every time they blow it out, relight it.

Joy is a deep kind of happiness. Often it is based on the love that we feel others have for us. Christians believe that God's love can give them a deep joy even in difficult times. Jesus said this about joy:

> **God the Father loves me and I love you. Now stay in my love ... so that my joy may be in you and that your joy may be full.** *(John 15:9–11)*

Reflection
Blow some bubbles, away from the children, and ask pupils to think of bubbly, joyful times. Burst some bubbles and ask them to think of difficult times. **Joy based on deep relationships can stay, even in those difficult times.**

Prayer (OPTIONAL)
Blow a bubble away from the children.

> **'Blow, breath of God, blow into our lives your endless joy.'** *(Based on a Kenyan prayer)*

AUTUMN FESTIVALS

You will need
>A card that says 'I can …'.
>Eight cards spelling out the words 'Thank you', and some fruits and vegetables (see Prayer, optional).
>Images of seeds and plants (optional): www.publicdomainpictures.net (search by 'seed' and 'plant') and www.thefruitpages.com/alphabet.shtml.

Introduction
Hold up the card and show the pupils one thing that you can do. Invite other members of staff and pupils to show something they can do. For example, 'I can hop'. **There are lots of things we can do, but there are also some things we can't do.**

Core material
Show the fruit and vegetables and ask who grew them. Talk with pupils about what the farmer does. Each action can be mimed by pupils.

➢ Ploughs the field.
➢ Sows the seed.
➢ Waters the seeds if it is dry.
➢ Gathers the crop.

All these things are done by the farmer, but the farmer does not actually make the seeds grow. Seeds would not grow into fruit and vegetables unless there was special life inside them that makes them come to life and grow. What the farmer does is give the seeds the right conditions in which to grow. At this time of year Christians celebrate Harvest Festival. They say 'thank you' to God, who they believe puts life into the seeds that makes them grow into the food people need.

Reflection
Ask pupils to think about tiny seeds and what must be inside them to push them upwards to grow into great plants. Show a series of images, if possible.

Prayer (OPTIONAL)
Eight pupils can hold the letters for 'Thank you' in a line. The words to go with each letter can be on the back of the card and be read out by the pupils holding them. Another eight pupils can hold the fruit/vegetables if they are used. (Check for any allergies.)

Thank you God for
Huge melons
Apples to crunch   **Y**ummy strawberries
Nice nectarines   **O**ranges to peel
Kiwi fruit from far away   **U**nusual fruit.

All Hallows' Eve

You will need
> Two balloons, one gold, one dark red.
> A pin and a polythene bag.
> An extract from a children's film or TV programme (optional).

Introduction
Please read the note headed 'Pastoral issues' (page 11). Play an extract from a children's film or TV programme showing an occasion where good triumphs. Alternatively ask pupils to think of examples of these. Explain that today's festival is all about a wrong being defeated.

Core material
Long ago, people in Britain came to meet together at this time of year to remember those who had died, at a festival called Samhain (pronounced 'sow inn'). Bonfires were lit as part of the celebration and also in the belief that the fires kept away evil. When Christians came to Britain they told the story of Jesus who taught that God's love is stronger than evil and that life is stronger than death. Christians believe in life after death.

For Christians this is a serious but not scary time of year, as they remind themselves of Jesus' teaching that God's love is stronger than all the wrong in the world. Halloween is the name given to 31 October and it is short for All Hallows' Eve. It is the day before All Saints' Day. For some Christians All Hallows' Eve is the day when they think about all the wrong in the world and the suffering it causes. They pray for those people who suffer and any who are frightened by Halloween. Some Christians have special parties that celebrate goodness.

Drama: Two teachers use the balloons, labelled 'Good' (gold) and 'Bad' (dark red), to have a mock fight. The balloons make contact with each other but not the people. Make sure that good eventually wins. There can be a running commentary.

Reflection
Put the red balloon in large polythene bag and burst it with a pin (warn pupils that you are going to do this). When it pops, ask them to think about the Christian belief that goodness and love are stronger than wrong and evil.

Prayer (OPTIONAL)
Ask pupils to draw a cross shape on the palm of one hand with a finger.

> **'As we make the sign of the cross, we remember that goodness is stronger than evil and life is stronger than death. We remember that love is stronger than hate and love will win.'** *(Based on a prayer by Desmond Tutu)*

You will need
> A narrow scarf in the middle of being knitted, using
> large needles and thick wool of different colours
> (just enough rows to be seen).
> White items including a white candle (unlit),
> and some music (see Reflection).

Introduction

Show the scarf being knitted and explain that knitting is increasing in popularity as a hobby. If possible, ask staff (any adults who work in the school) to show things they have knitted. If you do not have knitters on the staff, a parent may bring in examples.

Activity: Start with everyone standing.

- Sit down if you can knit.
- Sit down if you know someone who can knit.
- Sit down if you are wearing anything knitted.

Core material

Knitting joins things together; it joins lots of threads to make one garment. It can join lots of colours to make one scarf. Demonstrate with your knitting, by joining in a different colour. Alternatively, ask someone else to demonstrate.

1 November is All Saints' Day. On this day many Christians remember especially good and brave people of the past – the saints. Christians feel connected to other Christians; it's like being part of a big family. At this time of year Christians feel joined to the saints. The word 'knit' describes this sense of being connected. It is as if Christians, past and present, are 'knitted' together.

Note: If you have pupils of the Orthodox tradition they could be asked to share how they celebrate All Saints' Day, which is at a different time of the year.

Reflection

White is the colour for All Saints' Day. Create a white display – play some suitable music and ask pupils to bring items up one at a time, such as: a white flower, a white cloth, a white ribbon, a white unlit candle. Ask pupils to think about the good people they know who they feel connected to.

Prayer (OPTIONAL)

> 'Almighty God, you knit us together with the saints who have gone before. Help us to follow their example.'

All Souls' Day

You will need
A kite, or materials to make a kite
in the assembly (see Introduction below):
art straws cut to size, tissue paper, wool or string.

Introduction
Please read the note headed 'Pastoral issues' (page 11). Show the kite and talk about flying kites with the pupils. Alternatively, make a kite with the pupils:

➢ Make a traditional kite shape from art straws.
➢ Fasten the straws with sellotape.
➢ Glue tissue paper over the structure.
➢ Add a wool/string tail.
➢ Leave to dry while you do the next part of the assembly.

Core material
2 November is All Souls' Day. In some parts of the world it is known as 'the day of the dead', and is a time when Christians remember those who have died. In Guatemala people build huge kites and fly them. As they fly, the kites connect earth and sky and people are reminded that they are connected to those who have died. People feel joined to those they love who have died by their memories. Christians believe that there is a life after death. Although it is very sad when people die, All Souls' Day is not a sad day for Christians. All across South America, for example, people visit the graves of their relatives who have died, place flowers and say 'thank you' to God for their lives.

Reflection
Hold up the kite. **All Souls' Day sounds sad but it can be full of good memories.** Add a smile to the kite with a felt pen.

Prayer (OPTIONAL)
Pupils can write their own prayers on strips of paper, read them aloud then tie them to the tail of the kite. Or use the following to write down, read and add to the tail.

'Bless those we love.'
'Comfort people who are sad.'
'Thank you for those who have set an example by their lives.'

Remembrance Day

You will need

A paper poppy.

Large red paper petals and a small black circle for the centre of the poppy.

Introduction

Please read the note headed 'Pastoral issues' (page 11). Show the poppy and ask pupils why it is worn. **Poppies grew in the fields of Belgium where much of the First World War was fought. Few of the soldiers from that conflict are still alive, but poppies have come to stand for all those who gave their lives in war.**

Core material

Edward George Honey was an Australian. He served as a soldier in the First World War then worked as a reporter on a newspaper in London. Edward Honey thought about his time as a soldier and he remembered the day the war stopped. It was at the 11th hour on the 11th day of the 11th month in 1918. He remembered how people celebrated and danced in the streets – they were so happy that the war was over. Edward understood why they danced, but he did not want all those who had died to be forgotten. He thought that a time of silence was needed to remember those who gave their lives. Edward Honey wrote about having a time of silence in his newspaper, and soon the idea caught on and the king got to hear of it. King George V declared that from that time onwards there would a time of silence every year to remember those who died in the First World War. Twenty years later another war broke out – World War Two – and over the years since then many other people have died in wars. Each year silence is kept to remember them. It is held on the 11th hour on the 11th day of the 11th month, the time when the guns went silent in the First World War.

Listen to the Last Post and the Reveille (wake up). Both can be found on the website www.greatwar.co.uk/westfront/ypsalient/meningate/lastpost.htm. The symbolism of the Last Post can be shared. The Last Post (originally the soldier's 'goodnight', which reflects death) is followed by a short silence, then the Reveille is sounded (the soldier's 'wake up' call, which reflects resurrection).

Reflection

Prepare pupils for the two minutes' silence if you are going to take part in this. Alternatively, pupils' thoughts can be written on red paper poppy petals and these can be put together by pupils to make a poppy during the assembly.

Prayer (OPTIONAL)

Pupil prayers can be written on the paper petals, or the prayer below can be used. The poppy can be assembled as part of the worship.

> **'Thank you, God, for those who gave their lives so that others may live in peace.'**

Australia

You will need
> Images of Australia from the web (optional).
> A new bandage.
> A card heart shape.

Introduction
If possible play some Australian aboriginal music while the pupils enter. With the pupils, make a giant passport from paper. Explain that they are going on a 'flight'. Go through a typical take-off and landing routine (fasten your safety belts, etc.). Pupils can add sound effects. (For an alternative style of Introduction see page 26.)

Core material
Australia is a vast country and aboriginal people have lived there for many thousands of years. Europeans arrived about 250 years ago and occupied much of the good land, taking it away from the aboriginal people. The Europeans had little understanding of what the land meant to the aboriginal people. The land was not just where they lived; it was sacred to them, and the people felt a deep connection with it. Although they have been deeply hurt by what happened, however, in general aboriginal Christians do not seek revenge. Drama: Pupils can do a sketch about getting your own back.

Many aboriginal Christians see the wrongs of the past as wounds that need healing, and so they seek justice and reconciliation. These are long words. Justice means fairness; the aboriginal people want what is fair concerning their land. Reconciliation means bringing people together again in friendship. Many aborigines want friendship with people whose ancestors (great-great-grandparents) took their land. Revenge – getting your own back – is seen as only making matters worse.

Reconciliation is like a bandage helping a wound to heal. Drama: Pupils can act out someone falling over and a doctor/nurse applying a bandage to aid healing.

On the TV and in the playground we often see people 'getting their own back' (revenge). In the Bible it says:

> Don't hate people or take revenge, but love your neighbour as you love yourself.
> *(Leviticus 19:18)*

Reflection
Hold up the bandage. **Think of a time when you have fallen over and hurt yourself – how did the wound heal? Think of a time when you have been hurt inside (in your feelings) by a friend. We don't heal those wounds by getting our own back.**

Prayer (OPTIONAL)
Pupil prayers can be written down, read out, then attached to the bandage and wound round the card heart, to the words:

> 'May forgiveness heal our inside wounds.'

China

You will need
> A suitcase packed with items that suggest China or that would be useful if visiting China (optional).
> Images of China from the web (optional).

Introduction

If possible play some Chinese music as the pupils enter. Ask a few pupils to pull items out of the suitcase one by one. Can they guess which country today's assembly is about? (For an alternative style of Introduction see C1, page 25.)

Core material

China is a large country and huge numbers of people live there. Christians have been present in China for hundreds of years, but for many of those years Christianity was not welcomed in China. Instead of dying out, though, it quietly grew. Chinese Christians stress right behaviour. In other words, if you are a Christian your behaviour should show a change for the better. This is very practical, and Chinese Christians stress the daily difference that faith makes. The Bible says that faith must be shown in behaviour:

> What good is it if someone has faith in God if their actions do not prove it!
> *(James 2:14)*

Confucius, a great Chinese teacher, also emphasised right living, so it is natural for Chinese Christians to stress that their faith should lead to a change in behaviour. Christians find it easier to change if they think of specific things they do that could be done differently, rather than thinking in general terms such as 'be nicer', 'be a better person'. For example, people with quick tempers can show change by controlling their anger. Bullies can stop bullying. Christians believe that God can help people to make changes to their lives. Pupils could suggest the words for a modern song about changed behaviour. Use a nursery rhyme as a basis. For example, the following could be sung to 'The farmer's in his den'.

> I must not grab and steal.
> I must not hurt my friends.
> I mustn't fight and swear.
> I must not lie or cheat.

Reflection

What would you look for if a person's behaviour was to change for the better? What evidence would there be?

Prayer (OPTIONAL)

> 'Almighty God, may people see the evidence in us of behaviour that is changing.'

Latin America

You will need

   A suitcase packed with items that suggest Latin America or that would be
      useful if visiting Latin America (optional).
   Images of Latin America from the web (optional).

Introduction

If possible play some Latin American music as the pupils enter. Ask a few pupils to
pull items out of the suitcase one by one. Can they guess what today's assembly is
about? (For an alternative style of Introduction see C1, page 25.)

Core material

Latin America is the name given to an area that covers Central and South America.
(show images.) **It covers countries such as Mexico and Argentina, Brazil and Columbia.
Christianity in Latin America stresses justice and fairness, as in many of these countries
some people are very rich and some very poor. Persuading governments to change
wrong situations and setting people free from poverty is an important part of faith.**
Drama: Pupils can create a short drama on an unfair situation. Then ask the others
what would need to happen for the situation to be fair and just. For example:

➢ One person has a large plate of food, another has very little.
➢ One person has a big house and servants, another has one room shared by all the
   family, and the children have to work as servants.
➢ One person has lots of money, another has only a few pennies.

**Latin American Christianity is also a faith of celebration: fiesta and carnival. Music
and dance, drama and processions are part of faith. For example, Shrove Tuesday
(pancake day) is called Mardi Gras and there are a huge carnivals.** You could create a
joyful procession (conga) around the hall with some Latin American music.

Reflection

**Fairness, like peace, starts at home. We can all think of small things we can do to make
life fairer where we live.**

Prayer (OPTIONAL)

Make the prayer below into a Mexican wave using pupils at the front. Write each
word of the prayer on a separate piece of card. Each word is held up and taken
down in turn. This needs to be practised so that it happens fairly fast to create the
'wave'. Read it slowly afterwards.

   'Almighty God, help those who work for justice and fairness in the world.'

Africa

You will need

A suitcase packed with items that suggest
Africa or that would be useful if
visiting Africa (optional).
Images of Africa from the web (optional).
Folded paper.

Introduction

If possible play some African music as the pupils enter. Ask a few pupils to pull
items out of the suitcase one by one. Can they guess what today's assembly is
about? (For an alternative style of Introduction see C1, page 25.)

Core material

**Africa is made up of many countries, from Egypt in the north to South Africa in the far
south, from Ethiopia in the east to Senegal in the west. Christianity has been present in
Africa from the beginning. Jesus lived in Africa as a child; Mary and Joseph took Jesus
to Egypt to escape from Herod** *(Matthew 2)*. **An African called Simon of Cyrene helped
Jesus to carry his cross. Today there are Christian communities all across Africa. African
Christianity is about joy and being joined to others. The Bible talks about people being
joined together, like many parts of one body** *(Romans 12:5)*. **African Christians stress
being connected; rather than just being individuals, they feel part of a bigger whole.
This is called 'ubantu'.** Fold and cut out your line of people.

In our part of the world we often stress each individual. Tear off one person and
hold it up. **But in Africa it is the group you belong to that is important. Family and
friends really matter – belonging matters.** Glue the figure back on. **African Christianity
emphasises the 'ties' that hold communities together so people in churches have a
strong sense of belonging. They support each other, and look after each other if they
are in need. They also celebrate together.** If appropriate, learn an African Christian
song and add suitable drumming and other instruments. They are often danced!
For example, 'He came down that we might have love' (in *Jump Up If You Are
Wearing Red*, Church House Publishing) or 'We are marching in the light of God'
(in *All the Assembly Songs You'll Ever Need!*, Kevin Mayhew Publishers).

Reflection

Ask pupils to link arms and think about belonging, as a class and as a school. Add
names to the line of paper people.

Prayer (OPTIONAL)

**'Dear Lord, in our divided world people are separated from each other. Send your
Spirit to take away what divides us, and to make us one.'** *(Based on a prayer
from Uganda)*

South Korea

You will need

A suitcase packed with items that suggest South Korea or that would be useful if visiting South Korea (optional).

Images of North and South Korea from the web (optional).

Images of mountains (paper or projected, optional).

Introduction

If possible play some Korean music as the pupils enter. Ask a few pupils to pull items out of the suitcase one by one. Can they guess what today's assembly is about? (For an alternative style of Introduction see C1, page 25.)

Core material

The country of Korea, has suffered many tragedies. Sandwiched between the giants of China and Japan, according to a local proverb it is said that Korea feels like 'a shrimp between two whales'. Over the years Korea experienced both invasion and war, and this has led to its division into two countries, North Korea and South Korea. Both have very beautiful mountain scenery. Show images of Korea.

Many people in South Korea are Christians, and there are some very big churches. Prayer is very important to South Korean Christians. Some churches even have their own 'prayer mountains'. People can go to pray at the prayer mountain, where there is a building in which they can sleep and eat. They might meet others so that they can pray together; they might pray on the mountainside, looking at the wonderful scenery of their country. They might make a little shelter and pray by themselves with just a candle and a Bible. People do this because they remember that in the Bible Jesus, and other people, went up to mountains to pray, and prayer is important to Christians. Jesus went away by himself to a mountain to pray. *(Luke 6:12)*

Reflection

Show images of mountains, if possible, and ask the pupils to think about where they go if they want to be quiet and think/pray. Play some suitable music while they think, for example Richard Strauss's Alpine Symphony, or 'Mountain Symphony' by Zoo Series (Uni/Northsound).

Prayer (OPTIONAL)

'Korean prayer' is a style of prayer where everyone says their own prayer, aloud, at the same time. You need 'start' and 'stop' signals, as it can be quite noisy. Set a short time limit.

St Edward of England

You will need
> Enlarged illustrations (see page 87).
> Images of England and Westminster Abbey from the web (optional).
> Two strips of yellow/gold card to make into crowns.

Introduction
Please read the note headed 'Pastoral issues' (page 11). Follow the instructions on page 86 for creating the jigsaw. Ask some pupils to hold up each piece and say what it is and guess what it means. For example, what might a sword stand for?

Core material
As you read the following, ask pupils to select the correct piece of jigsaw and display it, fitting the pieces together one at a time.

1 **Edward was king of England between 1042 and 1066. He was a very gentle person and avoided wars wherever possible. He used to be the patron saint of England.** Put a large X through the sword.
2 **He did not ask his people for money (taxes) as many of them were poor. Instead he used his own money. He took Jesus as his example.**
3 **Edward passed laws to make life fairer for the people of England.**
4 **Edward built Westminster Abbey as a place to worship God. Many people visit the abbey in London every year. Even today, our kings and queens still wear a crown that contains gold from St Edward's crown.**

Reflection
Ask pupils what people remember about St Edward. Write key words on the crown card. Loop it into a circle and tape it. What words would pupils want on a crown if *they* could wear one? What would they want people to remember about them?

Prayer (OPTIONAL)
While the crown is flat, write prayers for justice and peace on it, suggested by the pupils. Alternatively, use the following:

> **'Almighty God, we pray for those working for peace in the troubled parts of the world.'**

Loop the strip into a circle and secure it.

St Edmund of East Anglia

You will need
> Enlarged illustrations (see page 88).
> Images of East Anglia from the web (optional).
> A jug of water and a bowl (optional).

Introduction
Please read the note headed 'Pastoral issues' (page 11). Follow the instructions on page 86 for creating the jigsaw. Ask some pupils to hold up each piece and say what it is and guess what it means. For example, what might the scales stand for?

Core material
As you read the following, ask pupils to select the correct piece of jigsaw and display it, fitting the pieces together one at a time.

1   **Edmund lived in the ninth century. When he was only fifteen years old he became king of the eastern part of England, known as East Anglia.** Show images of East Anglia.
2   **Edmund wanted to be a just king. He hated unfairness.**
3   **The east of England faces Denmark, across the sea, and Danish Vikings sailed to the coast of England and invaded Edmund's land. Edmund cared deeply for his people and tried to defend them, but he was captured by the Vikings.**
4   **Edmund refused to give up his Christian faith and died at the hands of the Vikings.**

Reflection
Ask pupils to suggest situations that are unfair. Talk about how unfairness makes them feel. Young King Edmund felt the same over a thousand years ago. That feeling can be used to help change situations.

Prayer (OPTIONAL)
In the Bible it says that justice should flow like water *(Amos 5:24).* **As you hear the water flowing from the jug into the bowl, pray silently about ways you can be just and fair at school and at home.**

> **'We pray for those who have power, that justice may be poured over your people like water.'**

You will need
> Enlarged illustrations (see page 89).
> Images of Vietnam from the web (optional).
> Three balloons (optional).

Introduction
Please read the note headed 'Pastoral issues' (page 11). Follow the instructions on page 86 for creating the jigsaw. Ask some pupils to hold up each piece and say what it is and guess what it means. For example, what might the number 6 stand for?

Play a game of hide and seek. The pupils can say 'hot', 'cold', 'getting warmer', depending on how close the seeker gets. **Hide and seek is just a game to us, but in certain places and at certain times it is played for real, and is very serious. Today's story involves a dangerous game of 'hide and seek'. It took place in a country called Vietnam.** Show images of Vietnam.

Core material
As you read the following, ask pupils to select the correct piece of jigsaw and display it, fitting the pieces together one at a time.

1 **Agnes lived in a country called Vietnam. She was an ordinary farmer's wife.**
2 **Agnes had six children, so life was very busy, with lots of hard work.**
3 **Being a Christian in Vietnam was dangerous at the time. Christians sometimes had to hide from soldiers. Agnes was very brave, often helping Christians the soldiers were looking for. One day a priest came to her house. She knew he was in danger, so she hid him in a deep hole where water was usually stored. It was dry at the time, so the priest did not drown!**
4 **Unfortunately the priest's hiding place was discovered. Agnes was arrested and she died in prison. St Agnes is remembered for her bravery.**

Reflection
All around the world there are lots of courageous people: farmers and doctors, factory workers and children. Bravery comes in many forms.

Prayer (OPTIONAL)
Three pupils hold up the balloons. Write a key word on each of them to stimulate silent prayer: ordinary, hardworking, brave.

St Andrew of Scotland

You will need
> Enlarged illustrations (see page 90).
> Three sheets of paper, one dark blue, two white.
> Images of Scotland from the web (optional).

Introduction
Please read the note headed 'Pastoral issues' (page 11). Follow the instructions on page 86 for creating the jigsaw. Ask some pupils to hold up each piece and say what it is and guess what it means. For example, what might the number 12 stand for?

Core material
As you read the following, ask pupils to select the correct piece of jigsaw and display it, fitting the pieces together one at a time.

1 **Andrew was a fisherman who worked in his boat on Lake Galilee with his brother Simon Peter.**
2 **Andrew was Jesus' first disciple (friend and follower). He was one of 'the twelve'. He brought his brother Simon Peter to see Jesus, who also became a disciple.**
3 **Andrew spread the Christian message during the first century, which was a dangerous thing to do at that time. Eventually Andrew was arrested, and like Jesus he died on a cross (a saltire or X shape).**
4 **An old story says that some of Andrew's bones were brought to Scotland. The Scots adopted Andrew as their special saint.** Show images of Scotland.

Make a paper St Andrew's flag with some pupils. Glue a sheet of white paper to the back of a dark blue sheet. On the front of the dark blue sheet add the saltire cross in white.

Reflection
Andrew brought his brother Simon Peter to meet Jesus and shared the friendship. Ask pupils to think of times when they have shared friends.

Prayer (OPTIONAL)
The prayer below can be written on the back of the Scottish flag.

> **'Thank you, Lord, for the example of Andrew, who brought Simon Peter to meet Jesus. Help us to share not only our things but also our friends with others.**

St Lucy

You will need
   Enlarged illustrations (see page 91).
   Sticky dot shapes.
   A tray of cakes for the staff (optional).
   White dress, red sash, card crown (optional).

Introduction

Please read the note headed 'Pastoral issues' (page 11). Follow the instructions on page 86 for creating the jigsaw. Ask some pupils to hold up each piece and say what it is and guess what it means. For example, what might the cake stand for?

Core material

As you read the following, ask pupils to select the correct piece of jigsaw and display it, fitting the pieces together one at a time.

1   **St Lucy was born in the fourth century in Sicily. She was known as someone who showed great courage. Her name means 'light'.**
2   **St Lucy's Day is 13 December. In Sweden on this day the oldest daughter of a family puts on a white dress with a red ribbon (sash) and wears a special crown. She takes cakes and coffee to the rest of the family. St Lucy's Day is the beginning of the Christmas celebrations in Sweden.**
3   **Lucy is a patron saint of blind people.**
4   **Braille is one way in which people who are blind can read.** Explain how Braille works. (www.afb.org/braillebug/braille_deciphering.asp)

Optional: A pupil can dress as St Lucy: white dress, red sash and card crown (see page 86) and take a tray of cakes to the staff. (Google 'St Lucy' for images.)

Reflection

Ask pupils to spend a few moments thinking about how we can easily take sight for granted, yet it is an amazing ability.

Prayer (OPTIONAL)

Show the Braille prayer (page 86) or recreate one using sticky dot shapes that can be felt with the fingers. Read the prayer.

   'Help us not to take sight for granted.'

Care-takers

You will need
- A blow-up earth ball (optional).
- A large notice showing the words 'Care-takers take care'.
- A large circle of blue paper (optional).

Introduction

Play 'spot the difference'. Make a few changes in the room before the pupils enter and see how many differences they can spot. Explain that the assemblies this week will be about making a difference; not changing something for change's sake, but in order to make the world better. Sometimes we can make a difference by changing one small thing.

Core material

Conduct an interview with your caretaker or cleaners about how they look after the school. Make pupils aware of the work they do and arrange for pupils to show their appreciation. Flowers or chocolates could be presented as a thank you. Agree beforehand with your caretaker/cleaner on one *small*, appropriate and safe thing pupils could do to take care of the school.

Christians believe that the world was made by God and given to people to look after. For Christians the story of Adam in the Garden of Eden applies to Christians today.

> **God put man in a beautiful garden and told him to farm it and look after it.**
> *(Genesis 2:15)*

Anyone can be a care-taker of the world, you don't have to be a caretaker. We can start looking after the world by looking after the place where we live and work.

Reflection

This reflection can be said a line at a time by pupils as the blow-up earth ball is passed along the line of speakers.

> **We can all take care and become care-takers.**
> **We can take care of the planet.**
> **We can take care of the part of the world we live in.**
> **Care is something that has to be *taken*. It doesn't just happen.**
> **Care-takers take care.**

Prayer (OPTIONAL)

Pupil prayers and/or the prayer below can be written or drawn on the blue circle.

> **'Lord, help us to enjoy your world gently.'** *(Based on a Yoruba poem)*

Penny change

You will need
> One pence coins that staff have brought in (see Introduction below).
> A soft chocolate bar.
> A plastic knife and a small basket.
> Information on a local charity.

Note: This assembly runs over two days.

Introduction
Arrange beforehand for staff to look for lost pennies at home and bring them in. Ask them to say where they found them. Talk about what you can buy in a shop for 1p. Ask an older pupil to cut a section of the chocolate bar that shows how much of the bar they think they would get for 1p.

Core material
One penny does not buy much. Pennies are worth so little that sometimes they are dropped and no one picks them up. They fall down the back of the sofa and no one bothers to look for them. Tonight, look for some pennies that have been dropped at home. Ask the adults if you can bring them to school. Don't worry if you can't find any. If you have a spare penny you can bring that in. One penny on its own may not be able to do much, but put together, pennies can help a local charity to change lives.

Reflection
With their permission, ask members of staff to empty the pennies out of their purses and pockets. Share some information about what a chosen local charity can do with this amount.

At the next assembly, choose some pupils to say where they found their pennies. Put all the pennies in a basket for the duration of the assembly. A penny display and information about the charity can be put up. **The Bible says that God looks at people's motives, why they give, not the amount.** *(Luke 21:1–4)*

Reflection
Use the nursery rhyme 'For the want of a nail' to communicate the role of small things. Pupils can recite this standing in a line. (www.rhymes.org.uk/for_want_of_a_nail.htm) Ask pupils to think about the difference small amounts can make (refer to the charity).

Prayer (OPTIONAL)
Have a large basket at the front. To suitable music, ask one pupil from each class to place the class pennies in a bowl. Hold up the basket.

> **'Father, we give our pennies to make a difference, knowing that you look on the heart and not on the amount.'**

Acts of kindness

You will need
> Go to www.actsofkindness.org.
> Droplet-shaped pieces of paper.
> A large sheet of paper.

Introduction
Ask staff and pupils to share stories of people who have been kind and the difference it has made to them. This can be in small or big ways. You could show an extract from a children's TV programme or film, such as *Charlotte's Web*.

Core material
Talk about kindness and the different forms it can take. Sometimes it helps to think in terms of opposites. Start by asking pupils to role-play a situation where someone is mean (you could decide the scenario). Follow by role-playing the opposite situation, where someone is kind. Create a kindness shower. Draw a large shower head on the paper and stick the droplets underneath. Add pupil suggestions concerning kindness to the droplets.

- **Smile more.**
- **Help someone.**
- **Play a game with someone new.**
- **Say please and thank you more.**
- **Share a toy with someone else.**

You will find lots of ideas on the website above. Some Christian quotations about kindness include:

> **Love is patient, love is kind.** *(1 Corinthians 13:4)*

> **I expect to pass through life but once. If therefore there be any kindness I can show … let me do it now.** *(William Penn, a famous Christian)*

Reflection
Ask pupils to think about showering other people with kindness. Can they think of something they could do today to show kindness to others?

Prayer (OPTIONAL)

> **'As we journey through life with others, give us the strength to be kind when we feel like being mean.'**

Change contracts

You will need
Blank certificates.

I _ _ _ _ _ _ _ will change _

_ _

I will need _ to help me remember

Signed

Introduction
We can all make a difference by changing one small thing we do. We all know that there are areas of our lives that we could change and improve. Say what you are going to change, and fill in your certificate. This can be a giant paper certificate or use an OHT or PowerPoint slide. Other members of staff or pupils might join with this.

I Jane Smith will change today by taking more time to appreciate

the world around me . I want to rush around less.

I will need a vase of flowers on my desk to help me remember.

Signed Jane Smith

Core material
The word 'change' is an important word in the Bible. It is often used in the context of changing behaviour. God asks people to change, but he does not expect them to do it alone. Christians believe that they can ask God to help them to change. They believe the Holy Spirit helps them.

Reflection
Invite pupils to think of one small thing they could change. You could have certificates for pupils to use in class if they wish to.

Prayer (OPTIONAL)
'Holy Spirit, as we seek to change, be by our side encouraging us, helping us, giving us strength.'

Change the planet

You will need
   Write 1,000,000 very large on a piece of paper.
   A hard-boiled egg.
   A school jumper.
   An empty plastic bottle.
   For more ideas visit www.reep.org.
   Words written on cards (optional, see Prayer).

Introduction
Show the number 1,000,000 and explain/give an impression of how big it is. How could people help the planet and save millions? Ask for pupils' suggestions and encourage them to write/draw them inside the noughts. The following scenarios can be presented with one pupil doing the actions that cost millions and another making the world-friendly suggestion.

➢ Screw up paper and drop it. **Don't drop litter – cleaning it up costs millions.**
➢ Drop a plastic bottle. **Recycle – it saves millions and they can be made into other things.**
➢ Drop a jumper in a bin. **Give unused items to charity shops rather than throwing them away – it saves millions. Clothes fill our dumps and the material could be reused.**

Core material
Christians believe that the earth belongs to God and needs treating with respect. In the Bible, the special book of the Christians, it says:

The highest heavens belong to God and the earth and everything in it.
(Deuteronomy 10:14).

Reflection
Hold up the egg and show the pupils how carefully it has to be held. Ask them to hold their hand as if they are holding an egg, and to imagine that the world is as fragile as the egg.

Prayer (OPTIONAL)
Explain that you have some left-over words. You don't want to throw them away – can the pupils recycle them into a prayer? Not all the words have to be used

Beautiful, treat, help, respect, you, us, a, world, God, us, with, have, to, it, given.

William Gilbert

You will need
  A magnet and objects to test.
  A compass.

Introduction
Hold up the magnet and ask pupils to tell you what it is. With the help of a few pupils, demonstrate what it can do. Can they predict what items it will pick up and what it will not?

Core material
William Gilbert was born in 1543 and lived until 1603. William was a doctor to Queen Elizabeth I. As well as being a doctor, William was interested in science. He studied how the magnet and the compass worked. He even began to investigate electricity. William Gilbert is not a very well known scientist, yet he was the first person to use the term 'electricity' and to study it.

In William's day English ships were sailing all over the world. Sailors used compasses, but they did not understand how they actually worked. William spent a lot of time discovering how the compass worked. To do this he had to understand magnets. William was unusual in that he did his own experiments rather than reading old books that were full of strange ideas. (One book thought garlic affected magnets, so helmsmen were not allowed to eat garlic at work.) William's experiments disproved some of the old ideas – including the one about garlic. His discoveries helped sailors move around the world more safely without getting lost. Demonstrate how you use a compass with pupils.

William believed that God had filled his world with things that people could explore. He believed that scientists should be able to discover the secrets of God's world, such as magnetism and electricity. William wrote down what he had found out about magnets, the compass and electricity, and other scientists found his work very helpful. They thought he should be applauded (clapped) for his work.

Reflection
Invite the pupils to give William a clap. As they do so they can think of the benefits of electricity and magnets.

Prayer (OPTIONAL)
Clap William as a scientist and then clap God for making a world for scientists to explore.

'Thank you, God, for scientists who show us a world of wonders made by you.'

Robert Boyle

You will need
    A bicycle and pump.
    Some small safe items (see Introduction below).
    A Bible and a globe or image of the world (optional).

Introduction

Have several pupils standing in a row, all but one of them holding something in their right hand (a piece of Duplo, a crayon, etc.). The hands should be curled so that the objects cannot be seen, and held out, including the pupil with nothing in their hand. Invite other pupils to guess what is in each hand. Now show what is in each hand. Did they guess correctly? Close the hands again. Can the pupils remember all the items? Ask what the pupil with the empty hand was holding. If the response is 'nothing', shake your head. Explain that the pupil had air in his/her hand. Today's assembly is about the man who discovered that air could be powerful and make things strong.

Core material

Robert Boyle was a scientist living in the seventeenth century (1627–91). When he was young he travelled round Europe and it was during this time that Robert first heard about a new invention – the air pump. Robert became interested and when he came home he started doing experiments on air. He worked on air pressure – the proper name for 'squashing' air – for many years. Robert discovered that this invisible thing we call 'air' can be powerful if squashed – but how do you squash air? You can't squash it just by sitting on it. The air just moves about and refuses to be squashed! Demonstrate. Ask for suggestions for ways of squashing air. You can squash air by forcing it in a small space. Demonstrate by pumping up a bicycle tyre. Air is forced into the small space of the tyre and it makes the tyre strong. The tyre becomes firm and can take a person's weight. Ride the bike a short distance. Robert Boyle's discovery helped people to use the power of air. He said that it was as if God had two books: one was the Bible, the other was the world. Through science, people can 'read' the book of God's world and find out about it and about God the creator. They can read the Bible to find out about God and his world.

Reflection

Ask pupils to think about the idea of reading the world like a book. What would they find on its pages?

Prayer (OPTIONAL)

'Thank you, God, for your two books:
    for all that we find about you and your word
    in the Bible and in creation.'

John Ray

You will need

Images of wild flowers from the web
(www.publicdomainpictures.net) (optional).
Card seed markers (optional).
A pot of play-sand (optional).

Introduction

Talk with pupils about jobs they might do at home, such as:

➤ Washing up.
➤ Tidying.
➤ Helping put away the shopping.
➤ Dusting.

Pupils might like to mime these jobs. **Today's story is about a man whose children helped him in his scientific work; they had a very unusual job to do at home.**

Core material

John Ray lived in the seventeenth century (1627–1705) in Essex. He studied hard and went to university in order to become a Christian priest. Earlier in his life, John had been very ill and while he was recovering he went for walks in the countryside. He was amazed at the plants that grew in an ordinary English field. Most people did not notice them, they merely trod on them as they walked. Ask what plants pupils might see as they walk in certain areas. Show images of wild flowers. **John became interested in studying plants and insects, but no one else studied them at the university, so he had to be his own teacher. John studied the wildlife around him and also travelled the world doing this.**

As John grew older he wasn't able to continue going out walking, so his children used to help him. The children did not dust or tidy, they did not wash up or clean the house, they went out and collected wildlife to help their father in his work. John wrote about the plants and insects he had seen. One of his books was on the subject of the wisdom of God in Creation. When he looked at the variety of plants and insects, John felt that God must be very clever to create them.

Reflection

Replay the images and take time to appreciate them. Alternatively, ask pupils to try to see a picture of their favourite plant in their mind.

Prayer (OPTIONAL)

Write prayers on the seed markers and place them in pots of play-sand. Flower pictures can be added to the sticks if you wish.

> **'Lord, sometimes we spoil the world you have given us, like toddlers breaking toys. Give us great respect for your world.'** *(Based on a prayer from Kenya)*

Adam Sedgwick

You will need
>   Some clean, safe rocks/pebbles.
>   A toy hammer.
>   A notebook.
>   Three bags.
>   Images of rocks from the web (www.publicdomainpictures.net) (optional).

Introduction

Put the rocks, hammer and notebook in separate bags. Ask a few pupils – one at a time – to come up and feel an item in the bag and guess what it is. Repeat this with all the items, which are clues to the scientist the assembly is about today. Can the pupils guess what he did?

Core material

Adam Sedgwick (1785–1873) was born in the town of Dent in Yorkshire, where his father was the vicar. Adam followed in his father's footsteps by also going into the Church, but the love of his life was rocks. He studied them and became a professor of rocks (geology). Show the rocks and ask pupils to describe what they see.

Adam walked round the country armed only with a hammer and a notebook. Show these items. **He carefully noted what he found out about rocks from his walks. Adam gave talks on rocks which became very popular. He was sure that it was possible to be both a scientist and a Christian. Once, when he heard someone grumbling and disagreeing with him on this, he took up a Bible and said that people should not be afraid of exploring God's world as scientists and using their eyes to see the world around them. It was like reading God's book of nature. Adam did other things in his life, such as working against slavery, and against injustice, but mainly he wrote books about what he discovered about rocks. In one of his books about rocks he wrote: 'May God guide you as you read this book' (paraphrased). After his death the people of his home town put up a memorial to him – a very large rock in his home town of Dent.** (www. yorkshire-dales.com/dent.html)

Reflection

If possible show a series of images of rocks of different types so that pupils can appreciate the beauty of them.

Prayer (OPTIONAL)

Pupils can join in the response:

>   **'For the rocks beneath our feet – Thank you, Lord.**
>   **For the beauty of the rocks – Thank you, Lord.**
>   **For all the hidden beauties of this world – Thank you, Lord.'**

Michael Faraday

You will need
   Things that work by electricity (for use by the teacher only).

Introduction
Place a series of appliances that work by electricity around the room (do not plug them in). Play 'I spy' on these items with the pupils. For example: 'I spy with my little eye something electrical beginning with T.' (Television).

Core material
Michael Faraday (1791–1867) came from a poor family, who could not afford to keep him at school. So he went to work at a bookshop. In his spare time Michael read the books in the shop and slowly got an education that way. He was really interested in books on science. One day Michael was given the chance to hear some talks by a famous scientist called Sir Humphry Davy. Michael carefully took notes at the lectures, wrote them up, bound them into a book and gave them to Sir Humphry Davy. A little later Sir Humphry developed problems with his eyes, after an explosion in his laboratory. He remembered the young man who had taken notes and made a book for him, and he gave Michael a job as his helper. From then on Michael worked as a scientist, first as Sir Humphry Davy's helper, then in his own right. He worked on electricity and discovered how it could be used to make people's lives better.

Every time we switch on the TV, radio, washing machine or vacuum cleaner we should remember Michael Faraday. He did the basic experiments on electricity that made all these things possible. But this work did not come easily; it only happened after thousands of experiments over many years.

Michael Faraday was a Christian. When he was asked to use his science to make weapons for war he refused. He turned down honours and lived quietly with his wife. He appreciated what was good in life, and he never lost his sense of wonder. He wrote to his wife: 'We are happy and our God has blessed us with a thousand reasons why we should be happy' (slightly paraphrased).

Reflection
Display this quote (credited to Faraday) as a focus for reflection:

   Still try, for who knows what is possible.

Prayer (OPTIONAL)

   'We believe in a world made for people to enjoy. We believe in a world full of riches for scientists to explore.' *(Based on an Indian prayer)*

What is truth?

You will need
> The 'Amen' chorus from Handel's *Messiah* (performances available online, e.g. YouTube) (optional).

Introduction
Play 'True or false'. Run a short quiz where pupils answer 'true' or 'false' to a series of questions. Make sure you have questions for all age groups. For example:

- **Grass is pink.**
- **12 times 12 is 144.**
- **Henry VIII had six wives.**
- **Feet is spelt 'pheet'.**

How do we know when something is true? Sometimes we can check for ourselves. For example, we could look outside to see if grass is pink. Other things are more difficult to work out.

Core material
The poet Steve Turner wrote this very short poem, 'What is truth?'

> **The truth**
> **is**
> **what's what.**
> **A lie**
> **is**
> **what's not.**

What is he saying about truth? Explore this with the pupils. You will probably need to read the poem several times. **The poet is saying that truth matches what really is, and lies don't. In the language of the Bible the word 'truthfulness' is 'Aman', and this is where the word 'Amen' comes from. The word 'Amen' means 'I think that's true' or 'I agree'. The Bible encourages people to think about what they say and make sure they are speaking the truth, because lies can do damage. In other words, people should think carefully about what they say 'Amen' to. For example, if someone is spreading rumours about another person, you don't have to believe it. Think, is it likely to be true? Does it match what you know of that person? Everyone needs to think carefully about what they say 'Amen' to.**

Reflection
Listen to some of Handel's 'Amen' from the *Messiah* while reflecting on the poem. Alternatively, listen quietly while the poem is read.

Prayer (OPTIONAL)
Learn to sing the word 'Amen' as a prayer, using the tune on page 92. (You may know it as the tune for 'Praise God from whom all blessings flow'.)

Conscience

You will need
> A cloud-shaped piece of paper.
> Chopped white paper or white confetti.
> Two paper plates with sad faces drawn on them.
> A toy boat or boat-shaped card.
> A PE whistle.

Introduction
Explain that today we will be performing a poem. Stand eight pupils in line and number them 1 to 8. As you read the extract from the poem 'Conscience' by Steve Turner (the lines have been numbered) each pupil does the action or holds up the item appropriate to that line. Practise once, then perform the poem.

1 **Does a cloud feel bad / When it blots out the sun?** (cloud)
2 **Does the wind feel sad / When it stops all our fun?** (sad face)
3 **Does the snow feel pain / When it gives us a nip?** (chopped white paper)
4 **Does the sea feel sick / When it shakes up a ship?** (toy boat)
5 **I feel sick / When I tell someone lies.** (hold stomach)
6 **I feel pain / When I don't apologise.** (arms huddled round chest)
7 **I feel sad / When I say a word that's cruel.** (sad face)
8 **And I feel bad / When I break the golden rule.** (head down)

Core material
Explain the 'golden rule' (see G4, page 48). Talk with the pupils about conscience. You may wish to improvise situations when conscience comes into play. **Some people ignore their conscience. After a while they no longer hear it. Others have a conscience that doesn't work properly and makes them feel guilty when they haven't done anything wrong. When we feel our conscience telling us to do or not to do something, we need to listen to it. We can check with others if we think our conscience is not working properly. The Bible talks about the conscience being like an inner voice** *(Romans 2:15)*. **It might 'say': 'You shouldn't be doing that', or: 'You should do something about that.'**

Reflection
Conscience can also be like a referee's whistle – warning us not to do something, or telling us to do something. As you listen to the whistle, think about a time your conscience made you stop doing something, or made you act.

Prayer (OPTIONAL)
As above. **As you listen to the whistle, say your own silent prayer about listening to conscience.**

The love of money

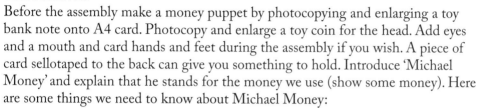

You will need
   Money puppet (see Introduction below).
   Money (coins).
   A plastic plate.
   Things to buy and sell.

Introduction
Before the assembly make a money puppet by photocopying and enlarging a toy bank note onto A4 card. Photocopy and enlarge a toy coin for the head. Add eyes and a mouth and card hands and feet during the assembly if you wish. A piece of card sellotaped to the back can give you something to hold. Introduce 'Michael Money' and explain that he stands for the money we use (show some money). Here are some things we need to know about Michael Money:

- **Michael is very useful, he can buy things we need.** Enact buying and selling with pupils.
- **People work hard to get Michael.** Enact with pupils.
- **Some people love Michael so much that they ruin their lives by wanting more and more, and they don't care what they do to get him.**

Core material
Read the extract from the poem 'The love of money' by Steve Turner, then talk about what it means.

I don't love money.	I don't love money.
It doesn't make much sense	It's such a fickle friend.
To fall head over heels	It promises the earth
In love with a pile of pence.	But leaves you in the end.

The Bible says that the *love* of money is the source of all wrong *(1 Timothy 6:10)*. **It does not say that money is wrong. Money can buy things we need, money can help people. Michael can be a good friend. He only becomes a bad friend when people misuse him. In the end money only buys certain things: it can buy toys and cars, houses and food, but it cannot buy friendship or love.**

Reflection
Drop some coins onto the plate and as they hear the sound ask pupils to think of the good things that money can buy. Repeat this and ask pupils to think about the way money can be a good friend or spoil lives. Money is a good friend but a bad master.

Prayer (OPTIONAL)

'Thank you, Lord, for money. (drop coin)
Bless it on its way as it buys bread for the hungry, (drop coin)
medicines for the sick, (drop coin)
and fun for the children.' (drop coin)

The golden rule

You will need
>   Some sweets.
>   A board game.
>   A toy.
>   A paper heart.
>   A key.
>   The golden rule – 'Treat others as you want to be treated' – written on gold
>   or yellow paper if possible.
>   Some key shapes on gold or yellow card (page 93).

Introduction

Perform this extract from 'The golden rule' by Steve Turner using eight pupils standing in a line. Practise the actions once, then perform.

1 **If you like sweets / Give sweets away.** (hold up sweets)
2 **If you like games / Let someone play.** (hold up game)
3 **If you like toys / Make sure you lend.** (hold up toy)
4 **If you like fun / Tickle a friend.** (mime tickling)
5 **If you like hugs / Hug someone new.** (hug self)
6 **If you like love / Then love them too.** (hold up heart)
7 **If you like freedom / Set someone free.** (hold up key)
8 **If you like you / Try liking me.** (point to others then self)

Core material

Talk with pupils about the poem. What is its message? Why does it have that title? **Steve Turner's poem is based on words from the Bible: 'Treat others as you want to be treated'** *(Luke 6:31).* **This is a saying found in many religions of the world. People call this the 'golden rule' because it is so important. Christians believe that people need God's help to keep the golden rule; it is difficult to keep by ourselves as we all tend to be concerned about what happens to us and forget what other people might be feeling or experiencing.** Setting people free can be setting them free from loneliness, etc.

Reflection

On the golden keys write some of the pupils' suggestions for how they want to be treated. **'I want to be treated ...'**

Prayer (OPTIONAL)

Pupils' prayer suggestions can be added to the keys. For example:

>   **'Help us to understand what other people are feeling and treat them as we want to be treated.'**

Peace

You will need
> Paper doves (see page 93).
> A hole punch.
> Wool or cotton thread.
> A world map or globe.

Introduction

Before the assembly photocopy and enlarge some dove shapes. During the assembly some pupils can help you cut these out. Make a hole in each one (teacher only) and thread a piece of coloured wool through. You can have some you made earlier as well. Introduce the dove as a symbol of peace. Read the poem 'Inner peace' by Lois Rock and talk about its meaning.

> **How can the angry world ever find peace?**
> **When will the gentle years start?**
> **I have no answer, so I shall begin**
> **to let peace grow in my heart.**

Core material

Ask pupils to suggest small ways in which they can bring peace to their part of the world. Write these on the doves. These should be specific and achievable. **I could decide:**

- **Not to argue with my brother over the TV, and find another way of solving the problem that is fair.**
- **Not to tease my little sister and make her lose her temper.**

In the Bible it says: 'As far as possible live at peace with all people'. *(Romans 12:18)* **Peace can start with individual people living peacefully with others. The 'gentle years' can start now.**

Reflection

Pupils place the doves on the map or globe while the teacher reads out the names of places where there is little peace. Ask pupils to think about the small ways in which they can make life around them more peaceful.

Prayer (OPTIONAL)

Sing the song 'Make me a channel of your peace' (*Come and Praise*, BBC) as a prayer. Alternative prayer:

> **'Heavenly Father, you call us to be peace-makers and bring your promised peace to others.'** *(Based on a prayer from the Pacific)*

Cecilia Flores-Oebanda

You will need
> A world map or globe or images of the Philippines from the web (optional).
> A basket of coloured ribbons.

Introduction
Mark out several 'safe squares' at the front of the hall. Play a game where one person is the catcher and a few others walk around near the safe squares. If the catcher tries to catch them, they can step into a safe square. Make sure the game is organised safely, with pupils walking not running. Today's story is about someone who made safe places for children.

Core material
In 2005 Cecilia Flores-Oebanda came from the Philippines to Britain to receive an anti-slavery award. Most people think that slavery ended about 200 years ago. But there are still forms of slavery today. (www.setallfree.net/cecilia_flores.html)

Cecilia was born into a very poor family in the Philippines. By the time she was five years old she was carrying a large basket of fish on her head, selling the fish to earn money for her family. She also worked on a rubbish tip to help them survive. When she grew up Cecilia joined a group of people who were fighting the government because they were treating the people badly. One day she was arrested for doing this, and sent to prison, where she was visited by a priest. He told her to look for a purpose in life, to do something to make a difference. From an early age Cecilia's faith had made her want to put wrongs right. Now she turned her attention to poor workers, particularly children. She started an organisation called Visayan Forum (VF), which helps children who have to work. VF provides medical services, a telephone help-line and safe houses for children to stay in if they run away from their employers. Wherever possible, Cecilia rescues those forced to work while still children, and arranges for them to get an education and gives them a new start in life. VF works hard to make people aware of the problem and to get laws changed so that children's lives are made better. Cecilia found her purpose. She made a difference. (www.antislavery.org/homepage/antislavery/award/cecilia2005.htm)

Reflection
Ask pupils to choose a coloured ribbon to remember child workers, and tie the ribbon in an appropriate place in the room. Ask them to think how they can make people more aware of the problem of child workers, for example by wearing something the same colour as the ribbon for one day.

Prayer (OPTIONAL)
Prayers can be written on the ribbons and tied somewhere they will be seen. **'For the work of VF we pray, and for all those who help child workers.'**

Cleophas Mally

You will need
> Safe items to represent different jobs (see Introduction below) (optional).
> Sticky labels and string.

Introduction

Ask a range of pupils – one from each year group – to stand up and say their name, age and what they enjoy doing. **We see childhood as a time for school and for playing. In some places this would be only a dream.** Another set of children, one for each age group, can read/say the following (write prompts on cards). They can each have an item to represent their job:

- **My name is Devaki. I am 5 and I clean floors.** (girl, broom)
- **My name is Eduardo. I am 6 and I pick fruit.** (boy, apple)
- **My name is Ulan. I am 7 and I look after the animals.** (boy, soft toy animal)
- **My name is Yusuf. I am 8 and I make carpets.** (boy, carpet sample)
- **My name is Lee. I am 9 and I work in a kitchen.** (girl, apron)
- **My name is Carla. I am 10 and I look after children.** (girl, baby doll)
- **My name is Dian. I am 11 and I work in a shoe factory.** (boy, trainer)

Core material

Cleophas Mally had a good life in Togo, Africa, where his father was a government minister. However, when Cleophas was eight years old his parents were forced to leave the country and he went to live with an uncle. Cleophas' uncle treated him badly. He forced Cleophas to work in the house from very early in the morning until he went to school, and after he came home from school he worked until all the adults had gone to bed. Through all this Cleophas talked to God, asking God to help him. He also thought of other children who were having a worse time that he was. Eventually Cleophas' parents were allowed to return to Togo. Things got better for him, but he never forgot what life was like for child workers. Cleophas works for WAO-Afrique, an organisation working to protect children in Togo and across Africa. WAO-Afrique works to find out what is happening to child workers, to let people know about it, and to try to get laws passed that will improve children's lives. (www.setallfree.net/cleophas_mally.html)

Reflection

Listen to the child workers again. Think what it would be like to have to work and not be able to go to school.

Prayer (OPTIONAL)

Write a prayer for each age group on the labels (one on each label). Fold the labels in half over the string to create a 'necklace prayer' to display. For example:

> **(5) 'May young children have the fun of playing.'**
> **(6) 'Free six-year-olds to go to school.'**

Chocolate slaves

You will need

4 large bars of Fairtrade chocolate that is 'traffik free'. See the good chocolate guide at www.stopthetraffik.org.

Images of work on a cocoa farm, for example from www.cocoatree.org (optional).

Introduction

Ask a group of children to take off the chocolate wrappers and fold each one lengthways into a thin strip. Tape the wrappers into circles to create links in a chain. Hold the chain up and say that today's story is about chocolate slaves (explain).

Core material

The chain is a reminder that thousands of children work on cocoa farms in West Africa. Some of the children have been forced to work. Here is what *some* of those children experience:

- They are not paid and some are treated badly.
- They sleep on the floor in crowded huts.
- They cannot go home and they are locked up at night.
- They have little food and work extremely hard for long hours.

For more information go to www.stopthetraffik.org. This site includes 'Chaga and the chocolate factory', the story of a child on a cocoa farm, which can be downloaded at no charge. There are also lesson ideas.

Many Christians are involved in the work to stop child slavery, as children are seen as particularly important to Jesus. Jesus said, 'Whoever welcomes a child in my name, welcomes me'. *(Matthew 18:5)* Here are some things you can do: Design a poster or T-shirt telling people about chocolate slaves, or buy chocolate that is 'traffik free'.

Reflection

Hold up the paper chain and ask pupils to think about the lives of the children who work on cocoa farms. A small stall of 'traffik free' chocolate could be set up at school for a restricted period.

Prayer (OPTIONAL)

Add pupil prayers on strips of paper to the chocolate wrapper chain. For example:

'Free children from the evil of slavery'.
'Lord, change the hearts of those who enslave children.'

Butterflies

Some paper butterflies (art straw with paper wings).
Images of butterflies from the web (optional).
Pupil dancers dressed as butterflies (optional).

Introduction
Butterflies are lovely creatures. They flutter through the air, landing very delicately on flowers. Sadly, butterflies do not live very long but in their brief lives they make the world more beautiful. Pupils dressed as butterflies can be dancing while you read this. Alternatively, demonstrate with the tissue butterflies on your hands.

Core material
It could be said that street children are like butterflies. They are beautiful, and they are constantly moving: finding places to work, places to sleep, on the pavement, in shop doorways, at the railway station. Sadly, life is so hard that some of them don't always live long. Butterflies is the name of an organisation that works with street children in Asia. In Delhi alone there are over 400,000 street and working children. Butterflies aims to help children, and also encourages them to help themselves by making their own decisions and getting involved in projects that will change their lives. As a result, the children have their own theatre, their own newspaper and their own bank. They do not wait for adults to do things that affect their lives, the children decide what to do to change their situation, with help from adults. For example, they might put on a play about the life of street children and take it around the area where they live. Butterflies is about children helping to change children's lives. (www.butterflieschildrights.org/)

Reflection
This week you could make your own class butterfly and display it. Spend a few moments thinking about something you could do as a class to make the school a better place for all the children. It does not have to be something big. Check with your teacher what you want to do and ask for adult help if you need it.

Prayer (OPTIONAL)
Ask pupils to choose a name from the list below and remember that name throughout the day. Each name represents a child worker or street child in Asia. Pupils can add details to their chosen name using their imagination, for example, 'Charu is six and likes to dance'. At the end of the day prayers can be said using the names.

Boys: Ajay, Bansi, Hari, Nandi, Tej, Ved, Darpak, Madhu, Rajiv, Vijay, Yash
Girls: Abha, Charu, Ela, Mala, Tanvi, Yamini, Usha, Jaya, Daya, Lali, Pari

CHANGING CHILDREN'S LIVES

Happy Child

You will need
> Images of happy children from www.happychild.org (optional).
> 12 brightly coloured paper plates.

Introduction

Talk about the word 'blessing'. What does it mean? **A blessing is something good that we wish for another person. For example: 'May you have lots of friends', 'May you have peace'. For Christians a blessing is about the good things people want God to give others.**

Core material

Some children in Brazil are very poor. They have no homes and no one to look after them. They live on the streets, sleeping on the pavements, and they are lonely and frightened. These streets are dangerous places, as the children might be hurt, go hungry and become ill. Show the images from the Happy Child website.

'Happy Child' is a Christian charity that was started in 1993 by John and Sarah de Carvalho. Sarah left her job in television to work with street children, and now Happy Child has 48 staff in Brazil and over 100 children live in seven different homes. The staff at Happy Child believe that children can be given twelve blessings:

1	Family		7	Education
2	Love		8	Prayer
3	Safety		9	Opportunities
4	A home/shelter		10	Hope
5	Food		11	Esteem
6	Someone to look up to		12	Time to have a childhood

Each of the blessings can be written on a brightly coloured paper plate and read out by pupils. Explain any difficult words.

Reflection

As the blessings above are read again, ask pupils to think quietly about the difference these make in children's lives.

Prayer (OPTIONAL)

This prayer is from a traditional blessing used by Christians.

> **'May God bless you and keep you. May God shine his face upon you and give you his peace.'**

The way of St Benedict

You will need
- At least one person to interview (see Introduction below).
- Images from the past and today (optional).
- A candle (in damp play-sand) and matches (teacher only).

Introduction

Often we think that 'now' is better than any time that has gone before. What we have now is seen as bigger, better and more convenient. There were, however, some things in the past that were better than what we have today.

Arrange for pupils to interview members of staff or parents about what they feel was better in the past (for example, a slower pace of life). Those being interviewed could bring in items to show (make sure all are safe if the pupils handle them). Alternatively, show a mixture of images from the past and today. Ask pupils to suggest what we might be able to learn from the past.

Core material

In this series of assemblies we are looking at something called 'The way of St Benedict' and how we might be able to learn from the past.

Benedict was born about 480 CE. As a young man he went to study in Rome but he was shocked at the behaviour of the people who lived there. As a result he decided to become a monk, and founded a monastery at Monte Cassino. Soon Benedict had twelve monasteries and later, after his death, more monasteries were opened across Europe. Life in the monasteries was quiet and orderly. People studied, worked and prayed and the monasteries became places of learning and peace. St Benedict lived in troubled times – there were wars and fighting – but while trouble and violence spread outside, peace and learning were kept alive within the monasteries.

There are still many monasteries of St Benedict today. One of the things we can learn from St Benedict and his followers (the Benedictines) is how to live more peacefully.

Reflection

Light the candle and talk about keeping the flame of peace alive by the way we live.

Prayer (OPTIONAL)

Light the candle as above.

> 'Lord, as the monasteries keep the flame of learning and peace burning in a world rocked by war, may we keep the flame of peace burning in our times.'

Sanctuary: refuge

You will need
> Soft toys.
> Some PE hoops or marked circles on the floor.
> An image of the Durham Cathedral door knocker from the web (optional).
> Music (see Reflection).

Introduction

Place the PE hoops on the floor or draw circles. Scatter the soft toys in and around the hoops. Ask a pupil to imagine they are a police constable and they have a certain number of seconds to 'arrest' the soft toys. They can only 'arrest' a toy that is outside a circle. How many can they arrest in the given time?

Core material

The word 'sanctuary' means 'place of refuge'. Many years ago, if a person was being chased by their enemies or in trouble with the law, they could enter a church and claim sanctuary. In the church they would be safe. Refer to the introductory game. **Some churches, such as Durham Cathedral, have a sanctuary door knocker. People would touch this to claim sanctuary. As long as a person stayed in the church they could not be arrested. (This right no longer exists.)**

Today, for many people life is very busy and they feel that they need to find a place of 'sanctuary'. They are not running away from enemies or the law, but just feel they need to get away from the busyness of life for a while and be quiet. Life was also busy in St Benedict's time, and his monasteries became places of sanctuary where people could find peace and meet with God. The motto of St Benedict is 'PAX', which is the Latin word for peace. Today some Christians make a sanctuary of peace and quiet in the middle of a busy life. They do not necessarily become Benedictine monks, but they learn from the monks about making a sanctuary in everyday life – a little bit of time for peace and quiet, away from the busyness of life.

Reflection

Play some busy music, then ask pupils to think about making time for quiet. Suggested music:

> 'The flight of the bumble bee' by Rimsky-Korsakov.
> 'Song of the Spirit' from *Adiemus II: Cantata Mundi* by Karl Jenkins.

Prayer (OPTIONAL)

Go to www.sacredspace.ie/ and scroll down to the days of the week. Search for a prayer you can adapt. Alternatively, whisper the following prayer:

> **'Thank you, God, for quiet, for all things hushed, soft and gentle.'**

Sanctuary: sacred space

You will need
> Images of sacred places from the web (optional).
> Different things to sit on, for example: armchair, cushion, upright chair.
> Music (see Reflection).

Introduction
Talk with staff and pupils about where they might go to be quiet. If possible, share experiences of being in sacred places from school trips. Show images of sacred places.

Core material
The word 'sanctuary' means 'place of refuge', but it can also mean 'sacred place'. A sacred place is where believers go to listen to God. For Christians, a sanctuary is not just a quiet place, it is somewhere they can go to talk to and listen to God. A 'sanctuary' can be anywhere. Ask pupils to demonstrate places of sanctuary (see below for examples) by sitting on the cushion or in the armchair. Choose pupils who will be comfortable with this. **A sanctuary can be:**

* **A favourite cushion in a corner of a room**
* **A seat in a garden**
* **The path to school or work**
* **An armchair.**

What makes a place sacred is the talking and listening to God that happens there. The Benedictines stress that you do not need to be in a big building to talk to God. A sacred place does not have to be a holy building; anywhere can be turned into a sacred place by what happens there.

Reflection
Play some quiet music and ask pupils to think about what they would have in their 'sanctuary' and where it would be. Suggested music:

> ➤ 'La Paix' from Handel's *Water Music*.
> ➤ 'Da Pacem Domine' from Taizé Chant for Peace and Serenity'.

Prayer (OPTIONAL)
Go to www.sacredspace.ie (as page 56). Alternative:

> **'Thank you, God, that our sanctuary can be anywhere and that you will always be there.'**

The door: virtue

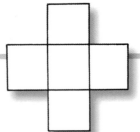

You will need
>A cardboard box with a lid,
>> such as an archive box.

Introduction

Before the assembly, cut down the sides of the box at each corner. Tape any raw edges and, if you need to, tape the base to stop it unfolding, so that the box will open out without undoing (see diagram). Show the pupils the box opened out and ask one or two to fold it back into a box again and put the lid on.

Core material

We are going to build a little cardboard house or 'sanctuary', just a pretend place that will help us to understand more about the way of St Benedict. To begin with we cut a door in one wall. You need to have a door or you will not be able to get in. Cut a door and fold it out. Draw a large V on the door. Asks pupils what the V might stand for. **The V stands for 'virtue', which is an old word that means 'behaving well'. The way you enter a room is by opening the door. The way you start thinking about life, for Benedictines, is by thinking about behaving well (virtue). St Benedict said this about virtue:**

* **Don't act in anger or bear a grudge.**
* **Don't deceive people.**
* **Don't wish someone 'peace' if you don't mean it.**
* **Don't turn away from someone who needs your love.**
* **Speak the truth in your heart and with your tongue.**

Enact some of the above. Suggest short scenarios for each one, which can be improvised. Alternatively pupils can give examples of each. Talk with pupils about how we might learn from what St Benedict said about virtue and why it is a good starting place.

Reflection

Draw a large V on flipchart paper and write up key words to think about, such as: grudge, deceit, peace, love, truth.

Prayer (OPTIONAL)

Pupils can make a 'doorway' using the fingers and thumb of an arched hand on the floor. Walk the fingers of the other hand through the door.

>**'Lord, help us to remember the door by thinking about our behaviour. Help us to take seriously your call to live well.'**

The floor: silence

You will need
> A carpet tile to fit in the 'sanctuary' box.
> Music (see Introduction below).
> Learn the BSL signs for 'quiet' and 'noise', see www.britishsignlanguage.com
> and www.learnbsl.org.

Introduction
Play some noisy music while the pupils enter, for example the 'Anvil Chorus' from Verdi's *Il Trovatore* or the cannons section of the *1812 Overture* by Tchaikovsky. Play some noisy games. Follow this by slowly quieting the pupils down. Ask them to get quieter and quieter until they are silent. Teach the BSL signs for 'quiet' and 'noise'. **We live in a very noisy world. There is always chatter and music and TV, and seldom do we experience silence.**

Core material
Yesterday we looked at the door of our 'sanctuary'. Today we are going to look at the floor. For Benedictines, silence is very important, as they believe that it is difficult to listen to God if there is lots of noise. Our piece of carpet stands for silence. If you stamp your feet on a solid floor they make a noise. Ask a pupil to demonstrate. **If you stamp on carpet it is much quieter.** Ask a pupil to demonstrate. Ask another pupil to place the carpet tile as the floor of the 'sanctuary'.

Say that you are going to do an imaginary walk round your home, stopping anything that might be making a noise. Ask pupils to make suggestions of noisy things you might find and do the stopping actions with you. (Remind younger ones that at home the adults turn off electrical equipment.)

➢ Turn off the radio.
➢ Turn off the TV using the remote.
➢ Put the dog outside if it is barking.
➢ Zip the lips (if you are making a noise).

St Benedict discouraged talking for talking's sake and gossip that might hurt others. He advised times of silence so that people could listen to others, listen to their own thoughts, and for believers, to listen to God.

Reflection
Encourage pupils to do the action for 'zipping the lips' and spend a few moments in silence.

Prayer (OPTIONAL)
Arrange beforehand for a pupil or member of staff to sign a short prayer, such as:

> **'God, thank you for quiet and time with you.'**

Alternatively, have a time of silence.

Wall 1: listening with the heart

You will need
> Things that make a noise, hidden from view.
> A short poem or tongue-twister.

Introduction

Do some listening exercises and see how well pupils can listen. For example, recite a poem, then see how much pupils can remember. Hide things that make a noise and ask pupils to guess what they are from their sound. Tell the pupils some information or a tongue-twister, then ask them to repeat it.

Core material

The next part of our sanctuary is the walls. The first wall is called 'listening'. Write 'listening' on one side of the box and use a book stand or some other means to make it stand upright. **In Benedictine monasteries a special type of reading and listening is taught. It is called 'Lectio Divina'. St Benedict called it 'listening with the ears of the heart'. This is a strange way of talking about listening because our ears are nowhere near our hearts.** Ask pupils to point to both. Ask one pupil to draw a heart – what do we think of when we see a heart shape? Ask another pupil to draw ears – what do we think of when we see ears? Ask a third pupil to draw a heart with ears on – what might this mean? **Listening with the heart means thinking about how we feel about what we hear, not just being able to repeat things, as we did earlier.**

Reflection

Now we have an opportunity to do some listening with the heart, or you can just listen if you want to. As you read the passage slowly ask pupils to do the following:

* **Be very still and quiet and listen very, very carefully. Listen as it is read again.**
* **If you hear something you want to think about, try to remember it. It might be just one or two words.**
* **Think about the words you have chosen. 'Chew' over the words in your mind.**

    Think about what is true, good or right in life and those things that are pure, lovely or worth admiring. If anything is excellent or worth praising – think on those things. *(Philippians 4:8)*

Prayer (OPTIONAL)

Those who wish to can go on to the next part of Lectio Divina: **Talk to God silently about the word or words that you have been thinking about. What might God be saying through these words? When praying in this way Christians remind themselves that God is loving and fair and would only ask them to do things that are loving and fair. They discuss their thoughts with people they know and trust.** Alternatively, pupils can pray silently.

You will need
> A radio-controlled car (optional).
> A flipchart.

Introduction

Encourage pupils to show you how the radio-controlled car works. **What else works in this way? Can the car decide by itself to do something different?** Alternatively, ask a pupil to pretend to be a robot. Role-play controlling the robot with verbal commands. Talk about the way a robot is controlled.

Core material

The next wall of our house is called 'free obedience'. With a pupil's help, lift up the second wall and tape it to the first wall, which should now stand upright. Write 'obedience' on the second side. Ask pupils to tell you what obedience is. They could enact people being obedient, improvising round certain scenarios, for example:

➢ The teacher asks you to help get equipment out for a lesson.
➢ The playground supervisor asks you to stop running but does not have time to tell you why (dangerous glass on the ground).

Benedictines choose 'free obedience'. This means that they choose to obey *freely* – they are not *made* to. It is not like being a robot or a radio-controlled car. We can choose to obey freely those who ask us to do what is *right*. (We can also choose *not* to obey those who want us to do wrong – and that would be a good choice.)

Reflection

As you listen to the sound of the car wheels whirring, think of something you are asked to do at school or at home. Think about doing it freely, without being made to.

Prayer (OPTIONAL)

Create a 'coat hanger' prayer. Pupils can stick/write the letters of the word 'OBEY' down the centre of a flipchart. The rest of the prayer can be written either side.

> Be with us, L**O**rd,
> As we seek to o**B**ey those who ask us to do right.
> Give us th**E** will to choose freely.
> May we know the jo**Y** that comes with obedience.

Wall 3: humility

You will need
> A safe plant in a pot.
> A five-step ladder.

Introduction

Show your plant and explain that in the pot is special soil called compost. **Compost is made of plants that have rotted down to create soil that helps new plants to grow.** If you have a compost bin at home talk about what you put in it. **Sometimes compost is called 'humus', which is another word for earth or soil. From 'humus' we get our words 'human' and 'humility'. Humility is about attitudes and how we think of ourselves.**

Core material

The next wall of our sanctuary is called 'humility'. With a pupil's help, lift up the third wall and tape it to the second one. **St Benedict thought that humility was really important. He likened it to a ladder of attitudes. Below are some of St Benedict's steps on the ladder** (adapted). As you describe the different attitudes, place a label on each rung of the ladder. **For Benedict these attitudes summed up what humility is. It is *not* letting others treat you badly.**

1 **Respect God.**

2 **Think about other people's needs and don't always want your own way.**

3 **Admit when you do something wrong.**

4 **Don't think you are more important than other people.**

5 **Don't grumble.**

Reflection

Think about which of Benedict's attitudes you think are really important. Compost helps the plant grow. Humility can be like 'compost for humans' – something that helps us grow good attitudes.

Prayer (OPTIONAL)

Say prayers for the five rungs of the ladder:

1 **'Great God, may we never forget that you are the maker of all that is.'**

2 **'Give us a thoughtful attitude that cares about others.'**

3 **'Help us to admit when we get things wrong, Lord.'**

4 **'Never let us forget that other people are important to you.'**

5 **'Give us a heart that does not grumble.'**

You will need

Four small round balloons of different colours.
A large table.
A short, safe stick for a cue.
Or a small toy snooker table (optional) or images of snooker from the web (optional).

Introduction

Place the balloons on the table and demonstrate with them how a cue is used in snooker (teacher only). **When I hit one balloon it rolls and hits others. They touch but just bounce off each other and then roll on. It is the same in snooker: one ball is hit and another glances off it or bounces off the side or drops in a pocket.** If you have a small snooker table then demonstrate. **Sometimes people behave like balloons or snooker balls: they bounce around off each other but don't really make contact. A group can be just a collection of individuals rather than a community.**

Core material

The last wall of our sanctuary is called 'community'. Explain what this means. With a pupil's help, lift up the fourth wall and tape it to the first and third one. **For the Benedictines, community is very important. A group of monks live together under an abbot and learn to get on together and support each other, even though they may all be very different. Living and working together is not always easy. Each monk has something to contribute and that contribution is valued. They are not like snooker balls, that just happen to be in the same place and occasionally meet and make contact. Our schools can also be communities where each person brings something to the larger group. They can be places where people really get to know each other and support each other.**

Reflection

Allow children to draw eyes and mouths on the balloons to turn them into people who look different (use safe, water-based felt pens). Other pupils can give the balloon people names and hold them in a line while you read the reflection.
'Sometimes we forget that we live in communities. We can each bring something different to make that community better. We can support each other through good and bad times.'

Prayer (OPTIONAL)

Individual pupils hold the balloons up.

> **'Father, forgive us when we behave as if we are just one person on our own.'**

Tape the balloons into a bunch.

> **'Remind us that we are joined to other people and we can celebrate together and sometimes face hard times together.'**

Display the balloons as a bunch with these prayers attached.

The windows and roof: hope

You will need
> Window shapes made of white sticky labels/paper.
> A coin.
> A large paper moon shape.

Introduction

In our sanctuary so far we have four walls, a door, and a floor with a carpet, but we have no windows. Ask a few pupils to stick the windows on each wall.

Core material

We have added windows because a sanctuary is not about escaping from the world but about finding a place to be quiet and gain strength in order to live and work in the world. So our sanctuary has windows to remind us of the outside world.

The next part of our sanctuary is the roof and this is called 'hope'. Place the roof (the box lid) on top of the sanctuary.

For Christians, hope is not something that *might* happen, such as, 'I hope my team wins at football'. When Christians talk about 'hoping in God' they are referring to trusting God for the future. Christian hope is a little like flipping a coin. When you flip a coin you can see one side but not the other. Demonstrate by playing 'heads and tails'. **If you can see the head side, you cannot see the other. However, you *know* the other side is tails. The same happens with the moon. We can only see one side, or part of it, at a time, but we know the rest is there.** (http://photojournal.jpl.nasa.gov/target/Moon)

We all need hope. We hope for a better world. For Christians this hope is founded in God. They believe that there is hope for this world and a life after death because they believe in a loving and powerful God.

Now our sanctuary is finished. We have learned a little from the past about living more peacefully in the world today.

Reflection

Look at images of the moon or watch a coin being flipped and think about your hopes for the world.

Prayer (OPTIONAL)

Write these words from Jeremiah on the paper moon and ask pupils to think about them silently. Or they can write their own hope prayers on Post-it notes and add them to the moon. The moon can be hung up and displayed.

> **'I have plans for you, plans for your good … I will give you a future and a hope.'**
> *(Jeremiah 29:11)*

Faith in business

You will need
> Fry's, Cadbury's and Rowntree's sweets, Fairtrade chocolate and a Terry's chocolate orange (see *You will need* sections from J2–J5, pages 66–69), in a shopping basket.

Introduction
Ask pupils to draw out the items from the basket one at a time and to guess what this week's assemblies might be about. **This week's assemblies are all stories about companies that first produced these sweets.**

Core material
Ask a few pupils to group the sweets into different companies. **All these companies were *originally* founded and run by Quakers (they have since been taken over by others). A Quaker is a type of Christian who worships and lives in a simple way.** (www.quaker.org.uk) Take the chocolate orange and open the segments. **We are going to use the 20 segments of the orange to explore some of the Quaker beliefs about running businesses.** Give some older pupils one segment each and ask them to read out one of the points listed below. (They can eat the chocolate afterwards, if not allergic or diabetic.) Some words or phrases may need explaining.

1 **Christian values should be applied to business.**
2 **Do not produce things that do harm.**
3 **Always be honest.**
4 **Respect each person.**
5 **Think about the good of others.**
6 **Go for high quality.**
7 **Business is work to be proud of.**
8 **Build trust.**
9 **Come to decisions by agreement.**
10 **Don't profit from injustice or dishonesty.**
11 **Pay a fair price to the producer.**
12 **Ask a fair price of the buyer.**
13 **Fixed pricing – no haggling.**
14 **Don't make money in a way that harms the community.**
15 **Money made is to be used for others.**
16 **Treat workers well.**
17 **Encourage good relationships.**
18 **Be careful with money.**
19 **Support each other in keeping Quaker standards.**
20 **Keep good accounts, never cheat.**

Reflection
Ask pupils to think of their favourite sweets. **Every time we taste sweets we can think of those Quakers who applied their faith to their business – and still do.**

Prayer (OPTIONAL)
Flatten the chocolate orange wrapper. Write down and say the prayer, and display it on the wrapper.

> **'Thank you, God, that faith can change any part of life, including business.**

Cadbury's

You will need
> Cadbury's Dairy Milk.
> Cadbury's White Chocolate Buttons.
> A sachet of Cadbury's Drinking Chocolate.
> Cadbury's Bournville.
> Images of Bournville village from the web (optional).

Introduction
Ask a few pupils to find the Cadbury's products from the shopping basket and hold them up. Ask what the difference is between these products, and open them to show the chocolate. Explain that there are different types of chocolate: milk, plain and white.

Core material
The Cadbury's company was founded by a Quaker called John Cadbury in 1824 and the business was carried on by his sons and grandsons. John sold drinking chocolate, coffee and tea as an alternative to beer, which was causing a lot of problems in society. Show the drinking chocolate. **At first no one knew how to make chocolate solid. Then, in the nineteenth century, a way of making eating chocolate was discovered. The Cadburys experimented with chocolate and created their own bar in 1847. Selling this new bar of eating chocolate made them wealthy. As Quakers, they believed that this money should be used to make a difference in the world. They looked after their workers, who had good working conditions, pensions, sports facilities, evening classes and medical care. The Cadburys also built new housing for their workers.**

Show the bar of Bournville and explain that it is also the name of a village. **The Cadburys were concerned about the terrible living conditions of workers at that time. Their houses were small, dark and overcrowded, with many families sharing one outside toilet. Water supplies were often dirty and there were few green spaces. As a result diseases such as typhoid and cholera spread, particularly among children. The Cadburys built a village for their workers just outside Birmingham and called it Bournville. The houses were airy and light and had plenty of room. Each house had a large garden so that the families could grow fruit and vegetables, and there was space for children to play. There was fresh water and good toilets and drains. Things began to change – people became healthier and there was less disease.** (www.cadbury.co.uk)

Reflection
Ask two pupils to role-play Victorian children, one from a slum and one from Bournville. They can talk about their different houses and the change in their lives.

Prayer (OPTIONAL)
Write the prayer on a large sheet of paper and ask pupils to glue Cadbury's wrappers around the edge. Display it for all to read.

> **'For shelter from the rain and snow, for homes to live in as we grow, we thank you, heavenly Father.'**

Fry's

You will need
Items of Fry's chocolate.
Some knitting.
A £5 note showing Elizabeth Fry (optional). Or find the image at
www.thebanknotestore.com.

Introduction
Display the knitting, the £5 note and the chocolate and ask what connects them.
Explain that today we are looking at a famous member of the Fry family.

Core material
The Quaker chocolate firm of Fry's was started by Dr Joseph Fry in the eighteenth century. He sold medicines and chocolate. One of Joseph Fry's relatives was Elizabeth Fry (1780–1845), who became a famous prison reformer. Elizabeth learned of the terrible conditions that many prisoners lived in and she wanted to do something about it. She visited women's prisons, where she found women and their children living in overcrowded, filthy cells – up to 30 in one room. They slept on the floor with no beds, mattresses or blankets. Ask pupils to imagine living, sleeping and eating in their classrooms with no running water, just buckets! Elizabeth was able to make changes: she made sure the women had clean clothes and bedding, a school and a chapel. She introduced sewing and knitting to keep the women occupied, and Quaker shopkeepers sold the finished products, giving the profits back to the women prisoners. Elizabeth encouraged them to make their own decisions in order to change their situation, and slowly conditions began to improve. Elizabeth worked to change prison conditions across the country and eventually some of her ideas were included in new laws governing prisons.

Elizabeth did not stop at improving prisons. She set up a nursing school at Guy's Hospital in London, and this scheme influenced a distant relative of hers called Florence Nightingale. She also introduced a visiting scheme to try to prevent people begging on the streets. A visitor would go to the houses of people in need and offer help if they were sick or had no food or money. More information on Elizabeth Fry is available from www.bbc.co.uk/schools/famouspeople/standard/fry/index.shtml#focus.

Reflection
Hold up the Fry's chocolates and ask pupils to think about the different aspects of Elizabeth's work: prisons, nursing, and helping those in need.

Prayer (OPTIONAL)
The £5 prayer:

> 'Her face gazes out at us from a £5 note. A very ordinary face, a mum who had eleven children of her own but still found time to change her world. Help us, Lord, to find time to help others.'

You will need
> Packs of Rowntree's Fruit Pastilles, Jelly Tots, Fruit Gums,
> Tooty Fruity Dominoes (optional).

Introduction
Ask a few pupils to find the Rowntree's sweets from the shopping basket and hold them up.

Core material
Rowntree's was originally a chocolate factory run by Joseph Rowntree and his brother Henry. Like the other Quaker sweet manufacturers the Rowntrees ran a family business that introduced good working conditions in their factories – long before such practices were usual. Rowntrees:

- Gave employees the weekends off.
- Cut the working day to eight hours.
- Built good houses for their workers.
- Supplied a company doctor and dentist.
- Paid good wages.
- Set up a pension scheme so that people would have money after they were too old to work.

Even this was not enough for the Rowntrees: Joseph Rowntree and his son Seebohm wanted to know what caused people to be poor. If it was possible to find that out, it might be possible to prevent it. (www.spartacus.schoolnet.co.uk/RErowntreeS.htm)

Explain what is meant by 'cause'. You can demonstrate this by setting up a domino rally with pupils, or some other simple cause and effect demonstration.

Seebohm Rowntree spent a lot of time finding out about the causes of poverty in Britain. He found that low wages were the main cause of poverty, and the very young and very old were the most at risk groups. He studied food to work out what made up a healthy diet. Joseph and Seebohm Rowntree used the profits from their business to set up a trust to continue their study of the prevention of poverty. The Joseph Rowntree Foundation continues this work today.

Reflection
Ask pupils to watch the domino rally and think about the need to find out the causes of poverty, and to prevent it, rather than just to help people when they are poor.

Prayer (OPTIONAL)
> 'Thank you, Lord, for the quiet work of people like Joseph and Seebohm Rowntree, and for the Rowntree organisation that is still today dedicated to finding the causes of poverty.'

Fairtrade chocolate

You will need
> Some Fairtrade chocolate (plus other Fairtrade goods if possible).
> A purse containing notes and coins (see Prayer).

Introduction
Show the Fairtrade logo (www.fairtrade.org.uk) and ask pupils what it means. Show some Fairtrade chocolate and other goods. **The idea of fair trade was started by churches after the Second World War. They sold products made by refugees in order to aid recovery.** Explain that we are going to explore what 'fairtrade' means, particularly looking at chocolate.

Core material
Chocolate is made from cocoa. The cocoa comes from the beans in a large pod that grow on a cocoa tree. The pods are cut, the beans scooped out and dried before being sent to factories to make chocolate. (www.cocoatree.org) Ask some pupils to read out the following:

* **Many cocoa farmers are very poor.**
* **They sometimes get little for their beans.**
* **The tools they need are expensive.**
* **The price goes up and down, so they never know how much money they will have.**

Fairtrade chocolate has been produced by farmers who:

* **Know they will get a fair price, which does not go up and down.**
* **Receive extra money for the community for projects such as building schools and hospitals.**
* **Work in safe conditions.**
* **Get education and training.**

Reflection
Ask pupils to hold up their hand in the symbol of hope that is the fairtrade mark. This is a hand for giving and receiving: giving good quality food and receiving a good price.

Prayer (OPTIONAL)
Say a 'purse prayer'. Take out different coins and notes from the purse and say what each amount can do. Pupils can hold the coin/note and say the words.

> **'50p: I help a farmer buy tools.**
> **£1: I help to pay for workers to receive fair wages.**
> **£5: I help to pay for their children to go to school.**
> **Thank you, God, for all those who use their purses to support others.'**

Luke Street assemblies

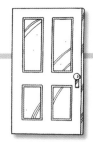

You will need
> 9 sheets of A4 card of different colours for doors
> (see page 94).
> A card street sign saying LUKE STREET.
> A Bible.

Note: This first assembly lays out the 'street'. At the beginning of each subsequent assembly a 'door' is opened and a story from Luke's Gospel forms the basis of that assembly. The story or passage from the Bible (Core material) can be photocopied and secured behind the door just before the assembly.

Introduction

Today we are going to make a street. We haven't got room to make the houses, so we are just going to have the doors. There are nine houses in our street. What do you think it is called? Take the pupils' suggestions, then show the street name and explain that it is a story-street. **Every house contains a story or a passage or some information. Each of the stories comes from the sacred book of the Christians – the Bible.** (You will need to remind pupils of this in each subsequent assembly.) Tape the left-hand edge of each door to the wall and secure the other side of the door. Make sure the doors are at pupil height. Draw a few rectangles on the doors to look like 'panels', and add door knobs and numbers, 1 to 9. Pupils can be involved in creating the street with the help of staff. Fix the street name to the wall.

Core material

Now we have our story-street. The stories behind the doors are very special stories for Christians. They come from part of the Bible called Luke's Gospel. Ask an older pupil to find Luke's Gospel in the Bible. **There are many different types of stories in our street: stories of poor shepherds and faithful women; stories of healing, and parties. Stories can show us situations like our own. They can give us advice on how to behave and what we should and should not do. In this way stories help us to live.**

Reflection

Ask the pupils to think of stories that have helped them. Share an example from your own reading.

Prayer (OPTIONAL)

Learn to sign the word 'Bible' (www.christiansigns.co.uk), then use the sign as part of the prayer.

'Almighty God, thank you for the stories in the Bible.'

Luke the writer

You will need
Images of the places mentioned from the web (optional).
A photocopy of the Core material and illustration (see page 95).
Paper rolled as scrolls and tied with ribbon.

Introduction
Ask pupils what a piece of good news might be. Arrange for a few of them to announce some good news, for example extra break time. **Our assemblies for the next two weeks are based on Luke's Gospel. This is a book from the Christian Bible. It is important to Christians because it tells the story of Jesus. The word 'gospel' means 'good news' and Luke's Gospel is the Christian 'good news' about Jesus. Each day we will knock on one of these doors, open it and see what is behind the door.** Ask a pupil to knock on door 1 and remove what is there (information about Luke and the illustration of a winged bull).

Core material
Our first story is not a story from Luke's Gospel, but some information about Luke himself. No one is absolutely sure who Luke was, but he is said to be the doctor who was a friend of St Paul and who went with St Paul on his travels. St Paul was a Christian who lived just after Jesus and he travelled to various countries telling people about Jesus. He went from Israel to Malta and Rome, and from Turkey to Cyprus and Greece. Show images. **But St Paul could not go everywhere, so Luke wrote down the story of Jesus in his Gospel, which meant that everyone could hear about it. His Gospel would have been written on scrolls and sent to local churches.** Show the scrolls.

Show winged bull symbol. **The symbol for St Luke is a winged bull. He was given this symbol because a bull is strong and serves by working in the fields. Christians believe Jesus was strong in love and served others.**

Reflection
Ask the pupils what message they would write on a scroll to make the world a better place. Some pupils can do this, with teacher help. The scrolls can be rolled up and tied with ribbon, then passed round the assembly until they reach the person who is going to read them out.

Prayer (OPTIONAL)
Prayers can be put on scrolls and passed to the reader as above. For example:

> 'Thank you for St Luke, who wrote down the story of Jesus.'
> 'Be with those who spread your message of love and justice today.'

K3 | *The announcement*

You will need
> A digital camera.
> Nativity costumes for Mary and the Angel.

Introduction

Introduce the word 'announcement' and explain its meaning. Make a series of announcements:

> ➤ Announce a winner.
> ➤ Announce a change.

> ➤ Announce some news.
> ➤ Announce a cancellation.

Ask a pupil to knock on door 2, open it and find the story.

Core material

This is the story of a very special announcement that is important to Christians. Later in the assembly we are going to turn it into a drama, so listen very carefully:

> **God sent the Angel Gabriel to a small town in Galilee called Nazareth. A girl called Mary lived in this town. She was an ordinary girl, going about her ordinary business. When the Angel Gabriel appeared, Mary was very frightened.**

> **'Greetings' said the angel. 'Don't be afraid, Mary. God is with you and has greatly blessed you. You are going to have a baby and you are to call him Jesus. He will be great, for he is God's son.'**

> **'I don't understand,' said Mary.**

> **'Don't worry,' replied the Angel. 'God is powerful. Nothing is impossible for him. God's Holy Spirit will make everything happen.'**

> **'I will do what God says,' said Mary. Then the Angel went away.** *(Luke 1:26–35)*

Two pupils can take the roles of Mary and the Angel (choose sensitively). Invite other pupils to be directors and to tell you what the characters should do and say. Take photographs of scenes of the drama. These can be printed and displayed later.

Reflection

The Annunciation is the story of God choosing a poor peasant girl, not a rich girl or a princess. We are not told that Mary was beautiful or intelligent or wealthy. It is character that matters.

Prayer (OPTIONAL)

Use an image or images of Mary, preferably from different cultures, as a focus for reflection (see art websites listed on page 96). Close with the prayer.

> **'Lord, you choose ordinary people and make them extraordinary. We are mostly ordinary but we know that you choose us to love and serve others.'**

The shepherds

You will need
> The chorus 'Glory to God' from Handel's *Messiah*.
> Images of shepherds (optional).
> A suitable box for use as a manger.

Introduction
Ask the pupils to think of some difficult jobs. These can be mimed, with others guessing the job. **Today's story is about some men who had a difficult and dangerous job. We need someone to knock on door 3 and find the story.**

Core material
At the time the Bible was written, shepherds had a difficult job. They took their sheep out onto the hillsides and looked after them. Shepherds had to find water and grass for the sheep to graze (eat), and they had to make sure the sheep were not harmed. There were dangerous animals on the hills: wolves and bears might attack the sheep. The shepherds protected the sheep, and that sometimes put them in danger. They stayed out on the hills all night, sleeping in the open, and earning very little for what was a difficult and dangerous job.

> **Some shepherds were looking after sheep on the hills around Bethlehem one night when they suddenly saw a bright light, and some angels in the sky. The shepherds were afraid – what was happening? An angel told the shepherds not to be frightened. The angels came with good news: a baby king had been born and he was to be found lying in a manger – an animal feed box. The sky was filled with angels singing: 'Glory to God in the highest and peace on earth, goodwill to all people.' The shepherds left their sheep and went to the town, where they found the baby, with his parents Mary and Joseph, just as the angels had said.** *(Luke 2:8–18)*

For Christians, Christmas is about good news. That good news was brought to poor shepherds. Other people may not have thought that the shepherds were important, but Christians believe that God thought that they were.

Reflection
Play the chorus from Handel's *Messiah* as pupils think about the good news being taken to poor shepherds. If possible, show a series of images of shepherds as the music plays (see art websites listed on page 96).

Prayer (OPTIONAL)
Sing a carol quietly as a prayer. Or ask pupils to suggest prayers that the teacher writes down, then pupils can place them in the empty manger.

> **'Give us the joy of the shepherds this Christmas.'**
> **'Help us to spread the message of the angels.'**

K5 Simeon and Anna

You will need
Name labels.

Introduction
Wear a name label and ask other people to volunteer to wear them. How did they get their names? Explain that some people have a naming ceremony. Children might like to share their experience of naming ceremonies. (For information on ceremonies, google 'naming ceremonies'.) Explain that names have meanings, and share the meaning of some names (see www.babynamescountry.com). Ask a pupil to knock on door 4 and find the story.

Core material
When Jesus was a very small baby Mary and Joseph had a special ceremony where Jesus was given his name. We call him 'Jesus', but in his own language (Aramaic) he would probably have been called 'Yeshua' or 'Joshua', meaning 'God saves or rescues'.

While Jesus was still a baby Mary and Joseph took him to the Temple in Jerusalem. While they were there a very old man called Simeon saw them with Jesus. He came over to them and said, 'This child will be like a light for all peoples.' Mary and Joseph were amazed, as Jesus was only a tiny baby. Soon afterwards an elderly lady called Anna came and saw Jesus. She also began to speak about him as someone special. *(Luke 2:22–38)*

Mary and Joseph returned to their home in the small town of Nazareth, where Jesus grew up: an extraordinary child in an ordinary town. No one would have guessed that this tiny baby would grow into a man that changed the world.

Reflection
Ask the pupils to write their own name with their finger on their palm and think about their potential.

Prayer (OPTIONAL)
Teach the BSL sign for Jesus (God and Human). (www.britishsignlanguage.com, www.learnbsl.org) Sign one or two words for each line:

Baby Jesus (2 signs)
Light of the World (2 signs)
Bring your love (1 sign)
To all people (1 sign)

Followers of Jesus

You will need
    Names of the disciples (men and women) on separate cards.
    A large strip of card for a friendship bracelet.
    Decorative stickers.

Introduction

Choose a pupil and ask them to choose a friend to join them. The friend asks another friend to join them. Keep on doing this until you have 18 pupils. Ask the friends about what they like doing together. **Today's story is about Jesus' friends and we need someone to knock on door 5 and find the story.**

Core material

Jesus chose 12 disciples *(Luke 6:14–16)*. Ask the pupils to hold up the 12 name cards.

Andrew	**Nathaniel** (also called Bartholomew)
Simon Peter	**Judas Iscariot**
James	**Simon the patriot**
John	**James the younger**
Matthew (also called Levi)	**Judas son of James** (also called Thaddaeus)
Philip	**Thomas**

Jesus and his disciples lived and worked together for three years. Luke is the only person who tells us that Jesus also had women disciples who followed him *(Luke 8:1–3)*. **Their names were:**

    Mary
    Joanna
    Susanna
    Many other women

Hold up the cards with the women's names. **It was unusual for a teacher in those days to have women disciples, but Jesus showed that women were important. These men and women were the beginnings of the Christian Church. They were ordinary people, mums and fishermen and working people. Jesus valued people for what they were, not what they had.**

Reflection

Ask the pupils to think about their friends and what they enjoy doing together.

Prayer (OPTIONAL)

Ask pupils to suggest a prayer (example below) that the teacher can write on the friendship bracelet. Pupils can decorate it with stickers. Tape the bracelet into a circle.

    'For all our friends, we thank you, God.'

I'm the greatest!

You will need
> A container of coloured water such as dilute blackcurrant squash and an empty jug.
> Plastic bricks and Duplo.

Introduction

Organise several competitions that will allow different pupils to win.

➤ A timed competition to fill a jug with coloured water using a spoon.
➤ A balancing competition to see how many plastic bricks can be balanced before they drop.
➤ A Duplo competition: who can build the highest tower in two minutes?

Clap the winners. Sometimes when people win a competition or a race they call themselves 'the greatest': the greatest swimmer, the greatest athlete, the greatest singer. These are all good things to be the best at, but there are other things to be great at. Ask a pupil to knock on door 6 and find the story.

Core material

Today's story is about an argument between some of the disciples.

> **The disciples were arguing about who was the greatest. Jesus sighed when he heard them, because he knew what they were thinking, but he did not tell them off. Instead he brought a little child to stand by him, and turning to his disciples he said, 'Whoever welcomes a little child like this, welcomes me and the one who sent me. If you want to be great, you have got to be prepared to be the least.'** *(Luke 9.46–48)*

This sounds a strange story to us, but the disciples would have known exactly what Jesus meant. In those days only women and servants looked after children and the jobs that women and servants did were not thought of as important. Jesus was saying that people who were willing to do jobs like that, jobs that were not glamorous and did not get noticed publicly, were really the greatest.

Reflection

Ask the pupils to think about spending time noticing and thanking the people who do the everyday jobs that normally we take for granted.

Prayer (OPTIONAL)

> **'It's hard, God, to do the jobs that don't get much notice. Help us to remember that service is greatness and that you notice.'**

Part of this prayer can be typed up in text-speak and displayed to make it easy to remember during the day.

> **'Fthr, hlp us 2 rmbr tht srvc is GR8ne$.'**

Advice about parties

You will need
> Party plates, dishes, cups.
> Party hats and streamers.
> Party invitations.
> Party music.

Introduction
Drama 1: Lay the table for a party. Invite some pupils and staff to be the guests. Arrange for the guests to argue over who is sitting where.

Drama 2: Ask pupils to enact taking party invitation cards to friends. Include giving an invitation to someone who is lonely and does not expect to be invited. (Choose sensitively who pays this part.)

Today's story is about parties, but first we need someone to knock on door 7 and find the story.

Core material
In Luke's Gospel we find that Jesus gives some very practical advice about parties.

> **When someone invites you to a party, don't grab the best place for yourself. Sit somewhere else, or it will look as if you are trying to make yourself too important. When you throw a party, don't just invite your friends. Invite some people who really need to go to a party, the less popular people, the lonely ones.** *(Luke 14:7–14)*

Jesus' advice is about attitudes towards other people. Sometimes people get very selfish and show off at parties, but Jesus' advice is not to make yourself the centre of attention. He also saw parties as a way of reaching out to others who may be lonely.

Reflection
Throw some party streamers, and ask the pupils to remember a party they have been to. Think about how Jesus' advice could have made it even better.

Prayer (OPTIONAL)
Play some children's party music and allow pupils to dance on the spot if they wish. Reduce the volume and say the prayer. Prayers do not *have* to be solemn.

> **'Thank you, God, for parties: for the fun, food and friendship. Help us to use them as a time for reaching out in friendship to others.'**

God's eyes

You will need
> A magnifying glass.
> Items to auction.
> A hammer for the auctioneer.
> A number of cards with words such as
> 'love', 'kindness', 'peace' written on them.

Introduction

The items for auction should be of varying values. Make sure all items are safe. Pupils can bid on behalf of staff. Make this fun, with people bidding against each other. (Monies can be returned in the staffroom.)

> **Here we have a lunch box valued at £1. What am I offered for it?**
> **Here is a notebook worth 50p. What am I offered for it?**

Ask a pupil to knock on door 8 and find the story.

Core material

Jesus spent a lot of his time teaching, and he was very popular with the people, but some religious leaders looked down on him. He was just a carpenter who taught ordinary people. Jesus said:

> **You like to make yourself look good to others. People see the outside, but God sees the heart and what you are like on the inside. There are some things that are considered of great value by people but they are worth nothing in God's sight.** *(Luke 16:14–15)*

In our auction we put values on things (50p, £1). Jesus taught that God's values are different. For example, he does not care what people look like on the outside and he is not impressed by riches. God values the really important things in life. What matters to God is what people are like on the inside.

Hold a second auction and people can bid for the cards ('love', 'kindness', etc.), but there is no upper limit – ridiculous amounts can be offered.

Reflection

Draw a heart on a large sheet of paper and fix the cards on and around the heart for reflection.

Prayer (OPTIONAL)

> **'Lord, you see and value the things that really matter – what we are like on the inside. Help us to do the same.'**

Easter baskets

You will need
    A small food basket.
    Some Easter food (such as chocolate eggs – *not* hot cross buns).
    A serviette.
    Tissue leaves and ribbons.

Introduction
Ask the children to remain silent for a minute or two. Ask them how easy they found this. Make an Easter basket with the pupils (see Core material) but do not tell them what it is. (Google 'Easter baskets' for more information.) The baskets are a Polish custom; Polish pupils could help with this activity. Ask a pupil to knock on door 9 and find the story.

Core material
Luke tells the story of Jesus' death on the cross on the day Christians call 'Good Friday'. Jesus was also buried on that day. Then Luke tells the story of Jesus rising again, on the day Christians call Easter Sunday. In between is Saturday, and Luke tells us that on that day Jesus' friends wanted to visit his tomb (grave) and take perfume and sweet-smelling spices, which was the custom at the time, but they couldn't because it was their special rest day of the week. They had to wait for the rest day to be over. *(Luke 23:44—24:35)*

Some Christians call this Saturday the 'Great Silence' or 'Holy Saturday'. It is called the 'Great Silence' because for three years the disciples had heard Jesus tell stories and teach – and now he was dead, silent. They thought they would never hear him again. Today on Holy Saturday some Christians go to church. The service is a sad one and people wait for the day to be over.

But it is not all sadness and silence. Some Christians bring baskets to church for the priest to bless. Show the basket. The baskets are lined with serviettes and decorated with leaves and ribbons. They are filled with Easter food that will be eaten on Easter Sunday. Pupils can add the Easter foods to the basket. Although Holy Saturday is a sad day for Christians, the baskets remind them of their most important belief, that Jesus rose from the dead and can still be a real but invisible friend.

Reflection
Have a time of silence while pupils think about times when they have had to wait but they knew that there was something good to wait for.

Prayer (OPTIONAL)
Add prayers that the pupils suggest to the Easter basket and display it. For example:

    'May we enter into the joy of Easter after the sadness of Good Friday.'
    'May we share the joy of Easter with others.'

The Advent journey: preparation

The series of assemblies that follows uses the idea of an Advent journey. Before the series begins you need to make some preparations, which can be an assembly in itself.

The Advent ring

Make an Advent ring with the pupils. Secure the candles in a bowl of damp play-sand. There should be three purple candles (weeks 1, 2 and 4), one pink (week 3) and one white (Christmas Day). Wind greenery around the *outside* of the bowl. Make sure the candles are tall and stand well away from the greenery. They should be lit by adults (with due regard to health and safety regulations). The Advent ring should be present at all the following assemblies and is not listed in the You will need sections.

Explain the symbolism:

➤ Circle – God who never ends.
➤ Greenery – everlasting life.
➤ Purple – sorrow and serious things.
➤ Pink – joy.
➤ White – purity and celebration.

Attach large rectangles of coloured paper to the walls, reflecting the colours of the candles, and representing the Advent journey. With the pupils, label the rectangles 'Week 1', 'Week 2', 'Week 3', 'Week 4' and 'Christmas Day'.

Reflection

Ask the pupils to think about getting ready for something important.

Prayer (OPTIONAL)

'Father, as we get ready for Christmas, help us to get ready on the inside.'

Note: The prayers in the four Advent assemblies draw on the language of the 'O Antiphons' (www.catholiceducation.org), traditional prayers said on the seven days before Christmas.

Alternative Christmas assembly

If the Christmas Day assembly (L5) on page 85 is not appropriate for your school, just light the fifth (white) candle and explain that Christians light this on Christmas morning to express their belief that Jesus is 'the light of the world'. Talk about the positive role of light in our world and demonstrate this with pupils.

In Jesus was life and that life was the light of all people. His light shone in the darkness and the darkness did not put out his light. *(John 1.4–5)*

The carol (page 85) can be listened to as a reflection or sung as a prayer. See also the assemblies on pages 72 and 73.

First week of Advent: hope

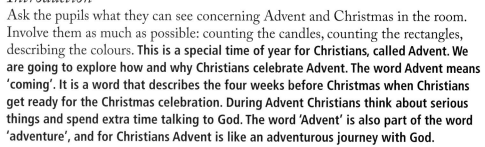

You will need
> Paper plates with sad faces and happy faces drawn on them.
> Tears made from silver paper.
> The word 'Hope' on an A4 piece of paper.
> Illustration of a rainbow (see page 96).
> An enlarged photocopy of the reading.

Introduction

Ask the pupils what they can see concerning Advent and Christmas in the room. Involve them as much as possible: counting the candles, counting the rectangles, describing the colours. **This is a special time of year for Christians, called Advent. We are going to explore how and why Christians celebrate Advent. The word Advent means 'coming'. It is a word that describes the four weeks before Christmas when Christians get ready for the Christmas celebration. During Advent Christians think about serious things and spend extra time talking to God. The word 'Advent' is also part of the word 'adventure', and for Christians Advent is like an adventurous journey with God.**

Light the first purple candle (teacher only). **The candle is purple, the colour of sorrow. For Christians this is the candle of hope. Christians celebrate the hope that one day all the things that spoil life will vanish. There will be no more sorrow, no war, and people will live together happily.** Invite a pupil to place the word 'Hope' on the Week 1 section of the journey.

Core material

Some older pupils can read the words from the Bible.

> **One day God will wipe away every tear from people's eyes. There will be no more death or sadness, no more crying or pain, for all those things will have passed away.** *(Revelation 21:4)*

Pupils can add the following to the Week 1 section: sad faces, silver paper tears, some happy faces, the reading.

Reflection

A rainbow (explain that it is a symbol of hope) can also be added to Week 1. A few pupils can colour this in with thick crayons while the rest listen again to the reading.

Prayer (OPTIONAL)

Three pupils can read the prayer, one line each.

(1) 'O Sun of our world,
(2) Shine your light on us,
(3) Give us hope.'

Second week of Advent: peace

You will need
> Paper doves (see page 93).
> The word 'Peace' on an A4 piece of paper.
> An enlarged photocopy of the reading.

Introduction

Light the second purple candle (teacher only). For Christians this candle is a reminder of their belief that Jesus came with a message of peace. He wanted Christians to work for peace in the world. Invite a pupil to place the title 'Peace' on the Week 2 section of the journey.

Core material

Talk about animals that don't get on with each other, for example cat and mouse, fox and chicken. Invite pupils to come out and mime pairs of animals (without touching). How might these animals behave towards each other? **In our world, it is not just the animals that fight. People fight. Nations fight and go to war. During the second week of Advent Christians think about peace and remember those places that do not know peace. They read these passages from the Bible.** Explain any difficult words.

> **One day a special king will come … he will be called 'The Prince of Peace'.** *(Isaiah 9:6)*

> **God's special king will be just and fair. He will defend the weak and the poor. In that day it will be so peaceful that the wolf will be able to live with the lamb, leopards and goats will lie down together, cows and lions will feed together in peace and no one will be harmed.** *(Isaiah 11:1–9)*

> **They will beat their swords into ploughshares and their spears into pruning hooks.** *(Isaiah 2:4)*

The writer wanted to describe complete peace, so he imagined the animals that would normally fight being friendly towards each other. Then he imagined weapons of war being turned into garden tools. Add the readings to the Week 2 section of the journey.

Reflection

Ask the pupils to think of weapons being changed into garden tools while Isaiah 2:4 is read again. Pupils can add doves (a symbol of peace) to the Week 2 section of the journey.

Prayer (OPTIONAL)

Three pupils can read the prayer, one line each.

> **(1) 'O King of the Nations,**
> **(2) Prince of Peace,**
> **(3) Give the world your peace.'**

Third week of Advent: Joy

You will need
> Coloured paper plates.
> The word 'Joy' on an A4 piece of paper.
> The carol 'Joy to the world' (www.cyberhymnal.org/htm/j/o/joyworld.htm).
> Musical instruments (optional).
> An enlarged photocopy of the reading.

Introduction
Light the pink candle (teacher only). **Today's candle is a different colour. Pink is the colour for joy and today is a joyful day for Christians. They know that Christmas is getting nearer.** Discuss what joy means (see A5, page 19). Joy can be a deep feeling inside or it can bubble up and be expressed in music, dance or laughter. Invite a pupil to place the title 'Joy' on the Week 3 section of the journey.

Core material
Talk with the pupils about what makes us joyful, and write these things on the coloured paper plates. A pupil can draw a joyful face on one plate. Pupils can fix the plates to Week 3 of the journey (use double-sided tape). Talk about getting excited when you have waited a long time for something and it has almost arrived, for example waiting for your birthday or a holiday.

> **The Jewish people had been waiting 400 years for God's special king. Christians believe that Jesus was that special king. Just before Jesus began his three years of teaching, a man called John the Baptist was telling people: 'Get ready, the king is almost here!' John told the people to prepare themselves for the king by saying sorry for what they had done wrong and changing how they lived.**
> *(Luke 3:1–6, 10–14)*

The third week of Advent is a time for rejoicing for Christians, because it reminds them that it is almost Christmas. It's almost time to celebrate the coming of the baby king. Pupils add the words of John to the Week 3 section of the journey.

Reflection
Play the first verse of the carol 'Joy to the world' and ask pupils to think about how they can bring joy this Christmas. If possible, give some pupils instruments. Play the carol again and ask them to improvise an accompaniment to the carol.

Prayer (OPTIONAL)
Four pupils can read the prayer, one line each.

> **(1) 'O King and Key of Life,**
> **(2) The joy of every heart,**
> **(3) Come and set us free from wrong,**
> **(4) Open the way for us.'**

Fourth week of Advent: love

You will need

> The word 'Love' on a card baton (rolled card or polyroll tube).
> The word 'Love' on an A4 piece of paper.
> The song 'What the world needs now is love, sweet love'
>   (optional).
> Paper hearts or Post-it note sticky hearts.

Introduction

Light the fourth (purple) candle (teacher only). **The candle is purple, the colour for kings. This is the candle of love. Christians call Jesus the 'King of Love'. Love is something that needs to be passed on.** Arrange several pupils as if in a relay race. Give the first pupil the baton with the word 'Love' on it. The pupils pass the baton (walking not running) but as they transfer it they have to think of some way they can show love to another person, and say it out loud. Ask a pupil to place the title 'Love' on the Week 4 section of the journey. The baton can also be added, with double-sided tape. Alternatively, listen to the words of the song.

Core material

Christians remind themselves that Ch ristmas is all about love: the love Mary had for Jesus and the love of God in sending Jesus. This is what they read in the Bible:

> **For God so loved the world that he sent his only son.** *(John 3:16)*

Ask a pupil to add the words of John 3:16 to the Week 4 section of the journey.

Reflection

Listen to the song quietly. Alternatively, write on the Post-it notes or paper hearts people who need love especially at Christmas. Pupils can add them to the Week 4 section of the journey.

- **Children who live in war-torn countries.**
- **People who may feel alone at Christmas.**
- **Homeless people.**
- **Those who will be in hospital or ill over Christmas.**
- **People who have to work over Christmas.**

Prayer (OPTIONAL)

Four pupils can read the prayer, one line each.

> (1) **'O Wisdom of God,**
> (2) **Strong yet tender,**
> (3) **You reach out across the world,**
> (4) **Teach us your way of love.'**

Christmas

You will need
> Words and music of the carol 'O little town of Bethlehem'.
> An empty crib and a blanket.
> A doll wrapped in a shawl.
> The words 'Light of the world' on an A4 piece of paper.

Introduction
Light the white candle (teacher only). **Christians light this candle on Christmas morning. It stands for Jesus. They call Jesus 'The light of the world'.** The carol can be played. Explain that this is a carol that is sung at Christmas by Christians. Add the title 'Light of the world' to the Week 5 section of the journey.

Core material
The carol talks of a town at night. Everyone is asleep and yet in that silent, sleeping town something incredible happened. Jesus was born but only a few people knew the importance of the event. Christians believe that people had waited a long time for this special child and that when he was grown up all their hopes would be pinned on him. Go through the words below with the pupils and ask them to create their own expressive actions for each line that will capture the meaning or express a key word: one action for each line. The signs need to capture the gentle nature of the carol. Add the carol to the Week 5 section of the journey.

O little town of Bethlehem	For Christ is born of Mary,
How still we see thee lie!	And gathered all above,
Above thy deep and dreamless sleep	While mortals sleep, the angels keep
The silent stars go by;	Their watch of wondering love.
Yet in thy dark streets shineth	O morning stars, together
The everlasting Light;	Proclaim the holy birth!
The hopes and fears of all the years	And praises sing to God the King,
Are met in thee tonight.	And peace to men on earth.

Reflection
Do the actions without the words reflectively while the carol is played.

Prayer (OPTIONAL)
Add the manger below the Week 5 section of the journey. While the carol is playing, pupils can place the crib on a table, line it with the blanket and place the baby doll inside. Prayers can be added to the manger, for example:

> **'Do not let us get so busy, Lord, that we have no room for you. May you find a home with us this Christmas.'** *(Based on a prayer from India)*

Appendix

The illustrations in the Appendix are photocopiable. They can also be downloaded free as a PDF file for printing from RMEP's website: www.rmep.co.uk/autumn

Notes for Autumn saints assemblies (D1–D5, pages 30-34)

Making the jigsaws
Jigsaws can be made during the assembly or drawn and cut out beforehand – it is up to the teacher.

> Take a large piece of thick paper or card.
> Draw a four-piece jigsaw on it.
> Cut out the jigsaw.
> Enlarge the relevant illustrations.
> Glue one illustration to each piece of jigsaw.

Instructions for making a St Lucy's crown (D5, page 34)

> Take a strip of card long enough to go around a child's head.
> Tape four white jumbo straws at spaced intervals to the outside.
> Add tissue paper to the straws as flames.
> Add tissue leaves to the base.
> Loop into a crown and tape.

Prayer in Braille (D5, page 34)

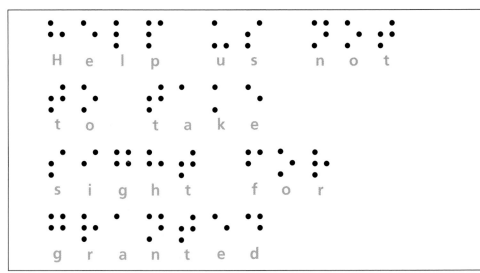

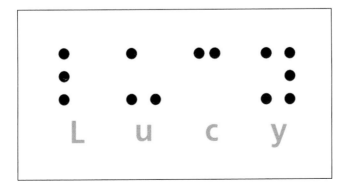

Tallis's Canon

Thomas Tallis (1505–1585)

Note: If you do not want to sing this as a round, change the final note to a semi-tone.

Outline of key (G4, page 48)

Outline of dove (G3, page 49)